INNER
TRANQUILLITY

ALAN JAMES was born in 1940. At the age of 28, he ordained as a Buddhist monk in London; after the death of his teacher, Kapilavaddho Bhikkhu, he completed his training in Thailand. In 1980 he co-founded the House of Inner Tranquillity, a meditation centre in Bradford on Avon.

As a result of the growth of the meditation centre and the increasing number of students who wished to train full-time, Alan established two monasteries (for monks and nuns respectively). The course of monastic training is firmly based in the model laid down by the Buddha in the Pali Canon, but adapted to a modern western cultural setting.

Today, Alan continues to teach the path to enlightenment, as well as directing the development of the monasteries and meditation centre. There is also a group under his instruction in London.

Alan lives in Wiltshire with his wife Christine.

by Alan & Jacqui James
A MEDITATION RETREAT
MODERN BUDDHISM

by Alan James
THE UNFOLDING OF WISDOM

INNER TRANQUILLITY

The Buddha's Path to Freedom

ALAN JAMES

BRADFORD ON AVON

First published 2001

Aukana Trust
9 Masons Lane
Bradford on Avon
Wiltshire
BA15 1QN

The Aukana Trust is a registered charity (No 326938)

Acknowledgements
The publishers would like to thank the **Fondation Jacques-Edouard Berger**, Switzerland, for kindly letting us use the cover photograph and **Rose Youd** for her invaluable publishing help.

Typeset in Bembo 11/13.5
Printed in Great Britain by Bookcraft, Midsomer Norton

Cover printed by Devenish & Co, Bath
Cover photograph © Jacques-Edouard Berger 1992

A catalogue record for this book is available from the British Library

ISBN 0-9511769-8-6

Contents

1

The Hidden Wisdom

A group of Japanese students invited a meditation teacher with an impressive reputation to a house where they met regularly to talk about Zen. Keen to hear what he had to say, they stressed that their enquiry was not casual; they wanted him to tell them how to meditate. He accepted the invitation and, after the usual greetings, began his instruction.

'There are a number of things you need to do to reach the goal,' he said. 'You need to develop equanimity about the successes and failures of daily life. You must develop generosity. You should develop reverence for all things, but particularly for the Buddha's teaching and its teachers. And you have to meditate correctly to realise that every single moment is reality itself.'

Standing up, he concluded, 'The whole process is like filling a sieve with water.' He bowed, and left.

Some of the students were upset, thinking that he had been telling them that their efforts were like trying to fill a sieve with water. One said that he could certainly vouch for that. He meditated now and then, and it lasted for a while—he was kinder to old ladies and children and cats—but it soon faded and he seemed no better than before. Another one agreed, saying that, yes, he read the sayings of the Zen masters from time to time, and it inspired him with thoughts of pursuing the meditative path but that too, like water in a sieve, ran away and he was left as badly off as when he started.

Some of them, a little more charitably, thought that perhaps he had been making a veiled allusion to something that could be found in Zen writings. They searched high and low for a reference to a sieve—but there was nothing at all relevant. They talked about it, on and off, for quite some time until all but one of them concluded that the master's reputation must have been exaggerated.

Undaunted by the opinions of her friends, one woman was sure that he must have meant something worthwhile. He surely was not laughing at them, as one had suggested. To find out what it was, she went to see the meditation teacher. Handing her a sieve and a cup, he led her to the nearby seashore where they stood on a rock, the waves lapping at their feet.

'Show me how you fill the sieve with water,' he requested.

She knelt and proceeded to ladle cupfuls of ocean into the sieve. The water covered the mesh briefly before disappearing through the holes. He said, 'Yes, that's exactly what happens if you try to fill the self with reality. You can never manage it.'

Taking the sieve from her, he hurled it out to sea where it floated for a moment, then sank.

'There. Now it's full of water—and will remain so,' he said. 'The way to see reality in every moment is not to try to ladle parts of it into the self, into your little life, into your cramped views, but to cast yourself totally into reality. That way there is no problem.'

*   *   *

We would all love to be able to immerse ourselves in the infinite. Some of us try very hard to do so. And yet we find it difficult, if not impossible. Why? Why can we not abandon ourselves?

There are of course many reasons—all can be grouped under the heading of conditioning from past behaviour and the influence of present circumstances. Some aspects of conditioning are more important in this respect than others and, from my observations over the years, there are a few conditioned attitudes that seem completely to block any progress towards letting go of self-view.

Many of us brought up in the West have learned to see injustice everywhere and this tends to prevent us from seeing what is under our very noses. For instance, some of us become distressed about the plight of minority groups, feeling that there ought to be legislation to adjust imbalances and perceived inequalities, that there ought to be, somehow, a common level. Typically, those of us with this problem frequently use words like 'unfair' and 'unjust' and believe that, no matter what the circumstances, no matter how hard people may have worked, it is still 'not fair' that some have more than others.

Many, whose idealism is stronger than their common-sense, are adamant that we should all be equal in every respect. There seems to be a conspiracy to neglect very real differences and pretend that they do not exist. Men and women should apparently be equal—and treated as such—in every area of human endeavour. It is like saying that there is no difference between an apple and an orange. Try telling that to the makers of cider or marmalade.

If we see injustice and inequality everywhere, we become aggravated and agitated to the point of outrage. We become provoked by the thought of racial differences and inequalities. We grow desperate at the threat of 'eco-disaster' and the reduction in bio-diversity as huge tracts of forest are felled and the green lungs of our beautiful planet are cut out.

Conditioned perception of this kind sees pollution everywhere. We see threats of nuclear war, of total starvation in third-world countries, of economic breakdown in the rest. We see corruption wherever we look. We worry and fret feeling that, surely, we must set these things right if there is to be sanity and balance in the world. Surely, we think, this cannot be the best of all possible worlds; it is not just, it is not fair; we—or, more commonly, they—ought to *do* something about it.

The perception, here, is always that other people are at fault. It is accompanied by anger and resentment—outrage—that they 'get away with' their harmful activities and a strong desire, a passion, that they 'should' be called to account and mend their ways. This desire can lead to personal action, as in various 'rights' groups, where outraged individuals take the law into their own hands and commit acts of violence on those with whom they disagree so strongly.

While all this may sound comfortably distant, few of us are immune from the tendency to believe that life 'ought to be' like this or like that. The tendency shows up most when things go wrong, when routines are broken or in times of great change. When was the last time someone behaved towards you in a way you thought was unjust? Said something to you that was not deserved? Pushed in front of you in a queue? Insulted you for no reason? Ran into your car? Made you redundant? Did you get upset at the injustice of it all? It is the same thing: it is someone else's fault.

Westerners react in this fashion remarkably often; it seems to be a function of our cultural conditioning. We are often concerned to police the behaviour of other people while paying little attention to our own. We fall into outrage and resentment, and even violent behaviour, on discovering things we believe to be wrong or unjust. It is as though we had no faith in the inner workings of the universe. Our conditioning in the West does not enable us easily to fill the sieve with water.

Most of us seem to be unaware of several natural laws that operate inexorably and efficiently to bring balance into both the natural and the ethical worlds. Our idealistically driven actions seek to adjust only the immediate and visible symptoms of imbalance or injustice, often in complete ignorance of the fact that life is a self-balancing system that needs little help from us. While there does of course need to be a legal system to constrain the behaviour of aberrant individuals and preserve harmony as far as that is possible, it can never do more than address the symptoms of imbalance. Laws hidden from the view of the majority not only address the symptoms; they also make some impact on the causes, as we shall see.

★ ★ ★

I read some time ago of the reproductive cycle of wild elephants in Africa. Apparently, their rate of reproduction varies greatly in dependence on the environment. In effect, elephants regulate the births of their young to suit the local conditions. If there is very little rain, and therefore a scarcity of food, they produce many fewer young than in times of high rainfall. Are elephants so highly intelligent that they undertake voluntary birth control? Or is the reason more fundamental?

Some years ago B F Skinner, the behavioural psychologist, performed a series of experiments with laboratory rats. His particular interest at that time was changes in behaviour patterns that arise from varying the population density. He found that groups of rats placed in overcrowded conditions developed some entirely new patterns of behaviour. They formed gangs and a few individuals became isolated or picked on by the others. Some became homosexual; others exhibited all the symptoms of depression or obsessive behaviour. They adapted to new conditions in a way that seemed to mirror some aspects of human behaviour in inner cities—which gave rise to some interesting new questions for the researchers.

Have you noticed how people in cities are very much more aloof from one another than those in rural areas? Is it because city folk really are 'stand-offish' and have no interest in others—or is there a natural law, a law of balance, in operation?

People need space and, if they do not get it physically, they have to get it psychologically. The only way to get psychological space when you are jammed up against six other people in the carriage of a London underground train is by cutting off from the physical environment. To preserve your personal space, you internalise and cease to react to pressures and contacts which, in a more open setting, you would probably complain about bitterly. Why is it, do you think, that people on trains read newspapers or books so often? Is it for the content of the book or the newspaper—or is it to preserve some psychological distance from their physical surroundings?

We all need personal space, whether physical or psychological. If we are unable to have one of these, we develop the other. If they both fail us, we break down. We adapt to our environment in an often-unconscious attempt to balance the pressures on us. There are a whole range of areas in which this occurs and, if unaware of what is going on, we may find ourselves troubled by the urges that arise and the uncharacteristic things we do.

In a supermarket, a harried housewife on a tight budget is tempted to slip something into her bag and walk through the checkout without paying for it. It would be very easily done, but she refrains. What stops her? The most common deterrents are fear of blame and fear of shame—two mental qualities the Buddha called 'the guardians of the world'. If someone who ordinarily would never consider acting in a criminal fashion does steal in this way, what stops him or her from doing it again? In most cases, the guilt that arises when reflecting upon the theft. Fear of blame and guilt, or fear of shame, form part of a self-balancing system. Discovering that certain kinds of behaviour produce discomfort, those actions are subsequently avoided. Behaviour is adapted dependent upon psychological pressures.

Each of us performs actions from which we experience results. If we harm others or steal, normally we feel guilt; we experience mental discomfort. If we speak harshly to others, we feel uneasy. If we indulge ourselves in sensual ways not permitted by society, we feel anxious about discovery, if nothing else. The man who runs off with his neighbour's wife inevitably feels guilty about it, at least for a time. We cannot prevent the reaction; we feel afraid of being found out—we feel guilty—or we feel shame. We may be able to squash the reaction down temporarily but it does not do much good; we know it is there. You could say, in a sense, that we have chosen to feel guilty. That 'choice' is made in ignorance of a natural law of action and result. With more understanding, we might have avoided the action in the first place. Our psychological reactions to wrong-doing tend to balance our behaviour and therefore the tenor of society itself.

Similarly, we can be said to have chosen the conditions of our current life. By our actions, we effectively 'choose' the circumstances of our next existence. Selfish action—action intended to boost our own sense of importance, our own egos, our own separateness—has results that are invariably unpleasant, often in this very lifetime and certainly in lives to come. Conversely, actions that place others first, that emphasise consideration and respect for life and liberty, that are not self-promoting, have uniformly pleasant results, both now and in future lifetimes.

Just as guilt may steer us away from performing certain actions, so a lifetime of hardship resulting from past misdeeds may throw us into reflection upon the meaning of existence. This can help us to learn from experience the hidden laws that govern much of our lives.

Experience is the key. There is a story about a lecturer who was touring Thailand giving talks on Abhidhamma, the higher teachings of Buddhism. Thousands of people would turn out to hear him discourse on his chosen subject. Keen to experience this phenomenon, a meditation student gained permission from his teacher to attend one of the talks. He listened in awe, stunned by the scholar's erudition and skill in presenting the difficult material.

Returning, he commented to his teacher, 'That was a remarkable experience. He's so learned, so clever, and so able to deal with the crowd. He's very impressive!'

The teacher smiled, and said, 'Yes, he does know a lot. In fact he knows everything about Abhidhamma—but that's all.'

The teacher went on to point out that the lecturer knew all the intellectual answers but was completely lacking in direct experience concerning the things of which he spoke. He could stun people with his encyclopaedic knowledge but, when it came right down to it, he was just a walking book. He had gained mere information from his studies, but no wisdom; his life was not radically changed from his endeavours.

The only way we learn is, in fact, the hard way. We do not learn the real lessons of life from books. We do not really learn from listening to other people. We learn the things that matter by living our lives, by experiencing the ups and the downs of normal existence. We agonise over difficulties and revel in good times. We learn through experience, through bitter defeat and fleeting success. Notice how easy it is to meditate when you feel that life is not quite right, when you have a problem. Notice how the urge diminishes when it is a beautiful day, when you do not have a care in the world and everything is pleasant. We are only driven to do something about our problems when we are aware of suffering.

Even here, the hidden laws are operating. It is no coincidence that we seek answers when things are difficult. Everything that is necessary for balance to be brought about is here, right now. There is a reason behind our feelings of need; there is a hidden wisdom behind the apparent disaster or problem. In fact, from this point of view there is no unfairness or injustice anywhere. Everything is perfect as it is. There is no need to take up arms in defence of this or that 'right' or principle.

Those of us who are experiencing a crisis have, as it were, chosen those very life-difficulties in order to learn. What do we need to learn? The origin of, and the escape from, the problems we face. We have to learn that actions do indeed have results; that how we live has conditioned our existing situation and will greatly affect how we become.

If we try to maintain our egocentricity, our selfishness, then we increase our frustration and suffering. It is like trying to fill a sieve with cupfuls of water. In contrast, we can learn that there is a reason for the things that happen to us. We can come to understand, through experience and through meditation, that life tends towards balance. Discovering that life is right as it is, we can let go of our precious separateness and throw ourselves into the ocean of reality. Doing so, we will learn wisdom and the art of graceful acceptance. We will learn far more than if we fight for our rights whenever anything upsets us.

Life is not just a random collection of events. There is hidden order in every situation. The hidden wisdom tends always to prompt every living being to develop full awareness of reality—here and now. If we choose to ignore those stimuli then suffering arises. In its turn, though, suffering prompts us to look for a way out of the distressing condition. In fact, suffering impels us towards awareness of reality. There is a movement towards balance. We are driven, by the hidden wisdom operating through life itself, to realise the truth of things here and now.

We do not have to fight all the injustice we believe we see in the world. Forgoing the battle for equality allows us to develop reverence for life as it is, warts and all, in the certain knowledge, born of experience, that everything in life is working for the best.

Giving up the struggle for external fairness and justice does not in any way imply indifference or cruelty toward those in need. Rather is it to acknowledge that a material utopia is forever impossible of acquisition. If we instead look each to our own development, we can aid the needy in a different, non-political, arena. One way to curb selfishness, thereby to move closer to reality, is to develop generosity, compassion and reverence for life.

Life *is* perfect as it is. Life works as it is. We overstep our limits if we insist that life should be one way and not another. If we wish to change things, we can with profit address our own behaviour, doing what we can to prevent ourselves adding to the negativity, the greed, the hatred, the frustration that is already in the world. We can learn to throw ourselves into the ocean of reality, or we can stay on the shore, puzzling about sieves and cups of water.

If we wish to immerse ourselves in reality as it is, there is an established method. The Buddha's eightfold path is a perfect way to do just that, though not an easy one. To walk that path means we have to let go of our tenaciously held views, customs and ideals. Indeed, as the Buddha himself said, we have to give up our beliefs to come to see life as it truly is.

Seeing things as they are, we realise that life is perfect. And, life being perfect, we realise that there is nothing to do. Even suspecting perfection, we may realise that we can relax, that life is, indeed, going in the right direction, that we personally do not have to worry about it. All we have to look after is our own behaviour, our own understanding. The world will look after itself.

2

The Highest Happiness

There are about six thousand million people in the world. Every single one is seeking happiness or, at the very least, trying to avoid unhappiness.

Whatever their skin colour, whatever their nationality, everyone searches for happiness. Rich, poor, well-fed or starving, young or old, of any religious persuasion or none, all people seek to be happy. We are all in the same boat and in this, at least, we are all very similar.

With six thousand million people on the same quest, it is clear from the many troubles of the world that ideas of happiness must vary considerably. The Buddha, when asked, said that happiness, wherever it is found and in whatever form it comes, is true happiness. He did not deny that some kinds cause misery to others and that others are blameless but, as we shall see, pointed the way to what he sometimes called the highest happiness.

Buddhism has been accused of being pessimistic, nihilistic and life-denying. The misapprehension has usually arisen on a mis-understanding of the Buddha's first noble truth, which states that everything in the world, without exception, is suffering.

'Suffering' is the usual word used for the Pali term, *dukkha*, which does not translate very readily into English. In defining *dukkha* the Buddha said, 'Birth is suffering (*dukkha*), decay is suffering, death is suffering. Sorrow, lamentation, pain, grief and despair are suffering. To get what one does not want is suffering; not to get what one does want is suffering.' The first noble truth does not deny happiness but, in its expanded form, points out that even the most sublimely happy states decay and die, which is *dukkha*, unsatisfactory, for we would like them to last. There is unsatisfactoriness, or suffering, inevitably associated with all conditioned phenomena, including happiness itself.

The first noble truth states the problem of suffering. The second noble truth states that suffering has a cause. The third states that all suffering can cease entirely. The fourth noble truth states that there is an actual path leading to the ending of all suffering. Buddha-Dhamma, the teaching of the Buddha, has the single objective of bringing its practitioners to the total eradication of suffering, to the cessation of *dukkha* called *nibbāna* or enlightenment. The elimination of an unsatisfactory condition can hardly be said to be pessimistic and one of the descriptions the Buddha occasionally used for *nibbāna* was 'the highest happiness'.

All who take up the practice of meditation seek happiness. Whatever their apparent or stated motivation, they feel there is something missing from their lives and that meditation will fill the gap or ease the pain. The whole purpose of this Meditation Centre is to allow individuals successfully to apply themselves to the task of overcoming distress by following the path laid down by the Buddha two and a half millennia ago. The monks, nuns and lay full-time trainees are committed to pursuing the path to the cessation of suffering and some of them pass on their knowledge and understanding to others who ask for instruction in the Buddha's teaching.

The path the Buddha laid down, the noble eightfold path, provides us with a definite plan to follow, an explicit set of directions pointing the way to increasing happiness—or decreasing suffering. Students follow a graded system of development handed down from teacher to teacher since the time of the Buddha himself and, if meditators apply themselves as instructed, they cannot fail to progress towards their goal. We find that increasing happiness is not at all a question of doing what we find immediately enjoyable, like indulging the senses through sensuality, ritual, art or poetry. In contrast, the path has much to do with the restraint of such indulgence and gradually calms the mind's restless pursuit of gratification.

To seek the constant and immediate satisfaction of bodily urges by way of the senses turns out not to be a very clever idea, as most realise. Less apparent, perhaps, is the fact that the same thing applies to mental longings for beauty, meaning and ceremony. Seeking satisfaction or happiness from such things merely exacerbates the craving for sensation and titillation, no matter how enjoyable and seemingly rewarding the sensual experiences are in the first place.

Those who indulge constantly—whether physically or mentally—find their palates become jaded and that they need stronger stimuli to get the same degree of satisfaction. The first order of business when seeking freedom is, paradoxically, to exercise restraint of the normally unchecked motivations towards indulgence.

At the most obvious level, restraint is developed by trying to maintain the five precepts. In their traditional form, these are:

'To undertake the rule of training ...
    ... to refrain from killing or harming.
    ... to refrain from taking what is not given.
    ... to refrain from unlawful sexual intercourse.
    ... to refrain from lying, slander, gossip and harsh speech.
    ... to refrain from intoxication through drink or drugs.'

In an extended form, trying to follow the spirit of the rules of training, this would include trying to curb all selfish desires that threaten to interfere in a destructive way with the lives of other living beings.

There is unquestionably a form of happiness to be found in destructive pursuits like hunting, fishing and trapping. Some human beings—mainly men it has to be said—even live for life-or-death battles against other human beings rather than animals; they live for fighting, for warfare, finding in these activities the stimulation they seek. However much of a thrill such activities provide, there is greater happiness to be gained from restraint of behaviour that harms others, whether animal or human, though it may not be visible until after the restraint has been applied for some time.

Women, no less than men, sometimes devote themselves to actions destructive of others' peace and welfare. A typical activity of this kind is to seek dominion in every relationship—and here some women use any means they can to achieve their objectives. We are all familiar with the image of the nagging wife and the hen-pecked husband but there are many other ways of dominating others including, for instance, 'emotional blackmail'. Even bright and positive qualities can be and sometimes are used with the selfish aim of superiority over others, of dominion, and, in these cases, it is the motivation behind such an activity that renders it suspect.

Harmful activities are popular; you have only to look to find many examples. Why? Why do people spend so much time and effort on behaviour that brings discomfort, harm and even death to other beings? The answer is simple. Those engaging in these pastimes enjoy it; they get a thrill out of it; they get a kind of happiness from it. Without question, there is a thrill in the chase, a thrill in the hunt and, equally, in subjugating others to your own will. Many people believe that life is only worth living if there is the excitement of danger, and danger is found most easily in activities which involve conflict, whether in the home, in the sports arena or on the battle-field. This is one of the modes of happiness.

There is also excitement and a kind of happiness connected with causing deliberate harm, well short of death, to another. While driving, a man was 'cut up' by a neighbour he knew slightly. Furiously angry, he dwelt on the wrong he had been done to the extent that he could think only of revenge. He bought some sulphuric acid and, in the dead of night, sneaked round to the other driver's car, which was parked on the street. Carefully, he poured the acid over the car and, the next day, gleefully told his workmates the story. It was plain that he derived much happiness from his nocturnal activity and that, sadly, he saw nothing wrong in what he had done, believing that he was fully justified. Being unaware of the law of *kamma*, he was likewise unaware of the likely long-term consequences of his action. For the time being, he was happy.

There is a kind of happiness much higher and more sublime than that which comes from the chase, from killing things and from harming others. It comes from abandoning such onslaught on other beings; it comes from restraining the urge to hurt and harm.

The happiness that arises from this restraint is based, in part, on lessened fear of others—you are not so worried that other people are going to get you before you get them. Also, there is less guilt, an easier conscience. If abandoning harming is augmented by positive efforts such as formally practising the meditations on loving-kindness or compassion, there comes to be much more friendliness towards all others and even genuine love untainted by any thought of personal advantage. The happiness arising from these activities is far more rewarding, far deeper and more sustainable than the happiness dependent on oppression and conflict.

The second precept is to undertake the rule of training to refrain from stealing or, more precisely, to refrain from taking what is not given.

Many today can testify to the trauma, the sense of outrage and intrusion that arises when their home is invaded by a thief. Someone caring only for his own gain breaks a window or forces a lock in the dead of night, sneaks into a house and makes off with worldly possessions prized by the occupants. A man, wanting new tyres for his car, puts a few bricks in the boot, drives around to find a parked car of the same make, takes off all its wheels and drives away with them. Another chooses instead to target commercial companies rather than private individuals and takes to shoplifting. All these thieves experience a level of satisfaction—of happiness—from their activities. There is the sheer adrenaline-rush, there is a belief that they are getting something for nothing (in reality it costs them very highly indeed, did they but know it) and there is the feeling of 'putting one over on people', of living outside the normal constraints of society. There is definitely a form of happiness in these anti-social and harmful practices.

There is, however, a demonstrably far greater happiness from not taking what is not given. Refraining from stealing is perhaps an obvious case. If, however, you also restrain yourself from the easy, but questionable, acquisition, there is a much greater happiness than that which comes from succumbing to it. If you refrain from buying that oh-so-cheap watch in the pub, you will be happier than if you bought it. If you refrain from eating your flat-mates' food without permission because yours is finished and you are not about to go without or go out to buy more, you will be happier than if you indulge your weakness. For the restrained of habit there is no guilt. There is also no fear of being found out, no fear of censure, no fear of prison and no fear of people generally.

As fear of being found out lessens there is less fear of others and an easier conscience. You begin to trust other people more—partly because you yourself are trustworthy. Your whole life takes on a totally different tone from that present when stealing is, if not a way of life, at least an habitual and unthinking indulgence. By keeping the second precept, you move up another rung on the ladder of happiness.

The third precept for the lay person is to refrain from sexual misconduct while, for the recluse, this becomes the rule of training to refrain from all sexual activity whatever.

It has often been said that sex makes the world go round and, if you look at almost any group of people in society today, it is hard to deny it. Sexual adventures and misadventures seem the one constant in almost every social group.

The precept in its lay form deals specifically with sexual activity that is damaging to other people and to oneself. Examples include the extremes of rape or sex with those under age or adultery and promiscuity. Trying to keep to the spirit of the rule of training, however, one would try also to minimise tendencies toward sexual discrimination and sexual harassment should they exist in one's character.

Many people know that sexual misadventures carry with them much happiness or, at the very least, excitement. They know—and usually ignore at the time—the concomitant perils, not only in being found out but also from the heartache and despair when things go wrong. The sex drive is very strong, leading people to ignore the constraints of law and custom and embark on adventures that, in retrospect, may make the offenders cringe with embarrassment. The thrill, the happiness at the time, is so great that it is no wonder that some find it difficult to restrain indulgence in this popular pastime. Keeping the precept, however stultifying it might at first appear, leads to a far more sublime happiness than wanton indulgence. Trying to conduct oneself in the best way on the sexual front gives a far greater reward than otherwise.

It seems to me that most of us find the fourth precept—enjoining restraint of gossip, slander and harsh speech—even more difficult to keep. People enjoy gossip; it makes them happy—or certain magazines, newspapers and various radio and television shows would not be as successful as they are. People enjoy slander—as long, of course, as it does not lead to a court case—usually not realising that this popular activity is damaging both to self and other. In contrast, a hungry and ruthless executive may knowingly undertake what he considers judicious character defamation of rivals, finding it works wonders for his 'progress' up the corporate hierarchy—and that makes him happy. Harsh speech—swearing, angry words, criticism and satire—provides delight and titillation for thousands upon thousands of people on a daily basis. Many of us would imagine life to be boringly bland without these forms of self-expression, never suspecting that they have a damaging effect on the minds of victim and perpetrator alike.

The peril in such unrestricted speech is manifold. Should we practise harsh speech on a regular basis, we soon develop a reputation for being critical, vicious and unfriendly. It is likely that we will not be trusted, particularly if our speech contains much exaggeration and falsehood. If we constantly run others down it should come as no surprise that others are likely to reply in kind. In short, harsh and unguarded speech destroys reputations—and that is to the detriment of all concerned.

Restraint of wrong speech of all kinds, including gossip, leads to a very different situation: one becomes known as moderate, balanced and courteous and is trusted more than someone who seems ruled by the need always to put others down. Being trustworthy, being known as someone of mild speech who does not tell lies or spread rumour and gossip, one's standing in the community improves, one has more friends, becomes happier and experiences less suffering.

The fifth precept concerns intoxicants. It is undeniably the case that intoxication through drinking and drugs does bring a kind of happiness. But it is clearly recognised by most people that what today are called substances of abuse—including alcohol, of course—potentially carry with them a huge and deadly overhead. If the habit should get out of hand, then the path to misery and degradation, even death, can follow in short order. The meditator is less concerned about the more obvious dangers of indulgence although, in a way, his problem is even more acute, for he needs all his mental faculties in perfect working order properly to observe reality and so dispense with the wrong view that leads to suffering. He or she is thereby constrained to avoid alcohol and drugs even in moderation for the interference with the meditation, even at low levels of inebriation, is quite enough to prevent clear seeing.

I know that some claim that 'soft' drugs such as cannabis can be an aid to spiritual insight. Drugs certainly do alter perception and can give glimpses of states of consciousness more desirable than the everyday. It is nevertheless true that, for someone intent on true freedom, they remain an undesirable indulgence that prevents any progress on the meditative path. Drugs, as artificial aids to 'meditation', chemically suppress the very aspects of mind and consciousness that the would-be meditator needs to observe to discover the truth of suffering and its origin. Through impatience or laziness, he is ignoring the very things he needs to examine in detail.

One of the truly debilitating effects of cannabis, incidentally, is that it saps the will-power of the user. Use the drug frequently enough and you are likely to experience severe difficulty in making decisions, choosing, instead, to let life just drift along. Sometimes users claim to be 'going with the flow' of life but in reality they are no longer in charge of their own lives. If they give it up, then everything changes for the better.

* * *

As we have seen, non-compliance with a precept is an obstacle to the meditative life and yet, precisely because the proscribed activity does bring a measure of happiness in its train, many at first fail to see the need to conform to these rules of training. A great many human beings delight in the hunt or in battle, feel good about getting something for nothing, find passionate thrills in sexual misadventure, enjoy gossip and slander and, need it be said, enjoy the fuzziness and removal of inhibition that inebriation brings. The trouble is that the happiness generated in these ways has a decided sting in the tail; the resulting dangers of excess are very real and can lead to dishonour, disease, poverty, imprisonment, confusion and even death.

It seems to me important that we recognise that those who do 'go off the rails' are seeking happiness or at the very least trying to bring about the alleviation of distress. They choose as their path to happiness actions that society finds unacceptable and, however obvious to others it may be that they are looking for satisfaction in the wrong places, they themselves cannot see it at the time. They may not be seeking for the best kind of happiness, but seeking for happiness, they are. Not knowing where best to look, they therefore deserve compassion rather than censure.

Where precepts are broken, where there is constant indulgence in selfish satisfaction, resultant feelings and perceptions in this life are painful—even if you 'get away with it' and are not found out—and the overall outcome is a downward trend towards an unfortunate rebirth. Such indulgence in inefficient actions, although at the time producing temporary happiness and thrills, carries with it danger that without exaggeration can be called a deadly peril.

Restraining anti-social and personally harmful activities, although more difficult than giving in to the urge towards immediate gratification, brings many benefits. One positive outcome is the absence of blameable behaviour and the resulting peace of mind. The individual has no fear of retribution from society—there is no fear of the law or of prison—and his conscience is clear; he has no guilty secrets. In addition, he is likely to be well regarded by friends and acquaintances and his reputation is good. In the longer term, behaviour based on restraint of selfishness leads towards a good rebirth in a state happier and more fulfilling than the present life. By the relatively simple expedient of keeping the precepts, the road to happiness can be assured.

* * *

Restraining anti-social tendencies provides a sense of freedom that has to be experienced to be believed. There is, however, greater satisfaction to be found. However much we refine our outward behaviour, we are still left with minds that, though free from guilt or shame, are nevertheless still unruly and subject to all manner of disturbance. To go further, to discover the happiness that lies beyond merely ceasing to annoy others, something else is needed: we need to address the discomfort or actual harm we cause ourselves. As with simple mundane behaviour, what some call morals and others ethics, restraint combined with attentiveness is the key. Both to see the extent of the problem of personal distress and to bring it under control, we need to apply restraint to the way in which we seek stimulation from our surroundings. This is known as restraint of the senses or, more accurately, restraint of the desire to seek gratification through the senses.

Sense-restraint is a more subtle form of the restraint of behaviour towards others. Those who keep the precepts may still indulge themselves in many different ways: one may overeat; another, listen to music excessively; yet another may be addicted to activity and exploration. While such immersion in sensuality causes little or no harm to other people, it unquestionably dulls the mind, rendering it unfit for the clear observation that forms the basis for the way to the highest happiness. In addition, this kind of indulgent behaviour tends to exacerbate the craving for sensory experience thus bringing dissatisfaction in its wake. Whatever way we look at it, constant sensory indulgence is a hindrance preventing further progress toward states of bliss beyond the usual. It needs to be restrained if we are to succeed in our quest.

For those under full-time training, food is often an issue of considerable importance. In the Theravadin tradition, monks and nuns may eat only one meal a day which, for those unused to it, is initially a practice difficult to accommodate. In the monasteries here, in Bradford on Avon, three meals a day are the norm: a light breakfast, a light lunch and a full meal in the evening. Even this is difficult for many at first. Gone are the huge helpings of lay life; gone are the snacks between meals. Learning moderation in eating, learning restraint of the desire for food, can be troublesome. However, perseverance brings success with considerable benefits that extend beyond simply fuelling the body. Worries about eating, about the quantity and quality of the food, eventually disappear and, in their place, there arises a relatively subtle sensory awareness. Because there is no over-indulgence, the perceptions become purer and cleaner, awareness of beauty increases and the mind is sharper and more alert.

Another area that poses initial problems is social interaction. Socialising engages all the senses in ways that most find very agreeable. Often there is a sustained assault on the sensory mechanism: drink in abundance, music, endless conversation, new and interesting people to meet, romance. Those who socialise a lot find it difficult to bring meditative awareness to bear on the finer thread of life that runs through everyday experience. The Buddha advised seeking solitude for a very good reason: the mind easily becomes dull and jaded if there is constant over-indulgence even in simple conversation. Being alone does not come easily to some meditators and there can be a long mental battle before the benefits of the more subtle mind are discovered. Some of those benefits are peace and tranquillity, contentment and the perception of beauty in the surroundings.

Sense-restraint gives greater sensitivity, greater awareness and a much greater sense of beauty. Self-confidence increases markedly as one feels more in charge of one's own life. As these things grow, there is an increase in the level of happiness one experiences as normal. It is very different from, and much more desirable than, the previous happiness arising from indulgence in the pleasures of the senses.

But it is possible to go further still.

* * *

Happiness gained through sense-restraint is a delight, yet even this is inferior in comparison with the happiness that comes from setting up mindfulness, the next sequential step in the meditative process.

To set up mindfulness in a systematic manner means trying to be aware, alert and fully conscious (though not self-conscious) of moving this way or that, of walking, standing, sitting or lying down, of any physical movement one should make. With sufficient application, there arises a level of consciousness not approachable in any other way. Refine the meditation by ensuring that the objects of awareness are 'right' in the sense of existing at the level of fundamental experience, rather than as mental fantasies, and you begin to develop such a subtle perception of life that previous awareness comes to seem clouded and dull.

Right objects of meditation include material objects, feelings, mental states and mental objects. Material objects, from the meditative point of view, appear to the senses as shape and colour or pressure and temperature. Feelings, we discover, are only of three kinds: pleasant, painful and neutral. Mental states include anger, sadness, bliss, happiness and so on that, in the West, we tend to identify as emotions. Mental objects include five hindrances; the five factors of faith, energy, mindfulness, concentration and investigation; seven 'wings of enlightenment': mindfulness, investigation, energy, pleasurable interest, tranquillity, concentration and equanimity—and many more.

Continued practice in setting up right mindfulness leads to an appreciation of life that is very different from what went before. It is as though you had been half asleep and not really in touch with what was happening in and around you. As mindfulness improves, zest arises and, with it, joy in ordinary living. Recognising the gains, there arises happiness far more satisfying than you had previously known.

Pursuing the correct course of meditation leads at the very least to the suppression of hindrances. The five hindrances are sensual desire (desire for experience through the senses); ill will or hatred (desire to stop or destroy sensory experience); sloth and torpor (dullness, laziness, unworkability of mind); flurry and worry (agitation, planning, tension, worry); and doubt. These are familiar to all meditators, who often find that one leads to another. The recognition of sloth or torpor, for instance, may lead to disgust or hatred of one's own inadequate meditation. That in turn gives rise to determination to succeed and great efforts are made to bring the mind under control. Excessive effort leads to agitation and tension so severe that it is difficult to continue with the practice, whereupon despair sets in ...

Right mindfulness allows sufficient clarity to find the middle path between the extremes of effort and concentration on the one hand, and blind faith and scepticism on the other, leading eventually to suppression of the five hindrances. Suppression of the hindrances is known as momentary or access concentration, depending on its strength, a delightful state that is sublime, calm and happy. It is so beautiful in comparison with anything experienced before that one wonders just why one had not troubled to seek for it earlier.

It is at this point of the path that the meditator is faced with a choice. He or she can follow either the *vipassanā* path, the insight path leading to the permanent end of suffering, or the *samatha* path, the calming path leading to intense peace and tranquillity here and now.

To gain utmost peace in the present, the depth of concentration has to be increased through one-pointed focus on a single object. This increases the depth of calmness and tranquillity until eventually the meditation seems to become 'fixed'—so quiet and stable that it cannot be upset. This state is known as a *jhāna* and there are in all eight of them, each one more sublime than the one before. The first four have as their object the world of form or materiality, colour and shape and, with each increase in concentration, happiness—here in the sense of tranquillity—deepens. The remaining four jhanas leave behind all trace of materiality, bringing satisfaction so sublime that it is difficult to describe. Eventually, for a few individuals, meditation can be deepened to pass beyond even the most sublime of the jhanas to arrive, fully conscious, at an extraordinary condition known as the cessation of all perception and feeling. Short of *nibbāna*, that is the ultimate happiness—a level of happiness not dependent upon pleasant feeling or, indeed, on any kind of feeling.

However sublime, none of these states can be made to last for more than a short time. The books tell us that seven days is the limit but, for most who attain the fixed meditations, a number of minutes or hours is probably more realistic than days. It takes work to maintain the skills needed to bring these deep states into being and, should those skills decay, the attainment is no longer possible.

There is another problem. *Jhāna* meditation does not eradicate suffering; it merely removes it to a distance while the meditation is practised. This means that, when the meditation stops, the untouched ignorance, craving and hatred have once again the potential to bring about great suffering. There is no ultimate security in concentration alone.

In contrast, insight meditation directly addresses the problem of the defilements of ignorance, craving and hatred. The priority of insight meditation is to observe the transience, unsatisfactoriness and non-self nature of all right meditation objects, rather than seeking calm in the moment. When done properly, this undoes wrong view and, eventually, eradicates ignorance, craving and hatred altogether and, therefore, all suffering.

Instead of applying the mind to developing increasingly deep states of concentration, the *vipassanā* meditator chooses instead to pay attention to the 'three marks of all conditioned phenomena'. These are transience (nothing lasts), suffering (every conditioned object is ultimately unsatisfactory as a base for lasting happiness) and non-self (no object, transient and unsatisfactory, is the permanent self of the me I wrongly believe to exist). Directly experiencing these marks, these aspects of everyday experience that are normally ignored, the wrong views on which suffering depends are gradually eradicated.

It is perfectly possible to develop insight using the concentration jhanas, the fixed meditations, as a base, and many teachers with good reason recommend that their students practise concentration first. Such a course demands freedom from external pressures and much time to oneself and, realistically, is best undertaken by someone in full-time training. Those unwilling or unable to take this step often prefer 'dry insight' meditation which tackles directly the ignorance at the root of the problem of suffering, without taking the time to develop deep concentration first.

Once access or momentary concentration has arisen, the mind is applied repeatedly to experiencing the transience of every object. In due course, the meditation takes on a new tone, one never known before and often described as achieving one's heart's desire. The transition is striking. From meditation that has been unremarkable and hard work, there is a radical change so that now it seems fulfilling, beautiful and sublime. So wonderful is it, so marvellous, so serene and yet so alert, that some make the mistake of believing that they must have reached the very end of the path, the cessation of suffering itself, *nibbāna*. It is in fact the very beginning of the true path, and there is much more to do.

This stage of insight meditation is known as 'direct knowledge of arising and passing away' because for the first time one sees directly, through experience, the mark of transience. This state, like any other, is a transient phenomenon and there are more such insights to come. Gradually, the meditation develops further, and deeper insight into transience, unsatisfactoriness and non-self begins to arise. With increasing understanding comes increasing happiness.

In time—and with much application—the meditator travels the *vipassanā* path to a point where certain knowledge arises. He or she becomes aware of complete and unshakeable confidence in eventual success in the meditation. The thought arises, 'I shall come to know the unknown'. Enough work has been done such that there can be no turning back, even if one should fall away from the training. When this happens, happiness increases. This, too, is happiness that does not depend upon feeling, serving to underline the fact that feelings, pleasant or unpleasant, are not the cause of happiness even though they seem so important to the untrained.

Finally, on the *vipassanā* path, we come to the total cessation of *dukkha*. We come to the ultimate knowledge. We come to *nibbāna*, enlightenment, the cessation of all ignorance, craving and hatred. This is the highest happiness, and it is towards this that the whole teaching is aimed. This is the goal, whether one starts with *samatha*, calming meditation, or *vipassanā*, insight.

The Buddha's teaching goes in only one direction and that is towards the ending of all suffering that he sometimes called the highest happiness. It may be difficult along the way but, for everyone who is practising in the correct manner, suffering reduces—happiness increases—slowly, gradually, steadily, but definitely. The purpose of a place like this Meditation Centre is to lead you toward increasing happiness at the fastest pace you can stand.

3

A Chance of Freedom

Knowing you meditate and might be interested, a friend shows you a philosophy exam paper he has found. The very first question is 'What is freedom?' The multiple-choice answers are as follows:

(a) To do what you want, when you want.
(b) To do what you want, as long as it does not interfere with another's freedom.
(c) Neither of the above.

You feel you should know the answer, but which one do you choose? It takes some thought; the question is as old as mankind. Let us look at the options.

Is the answer (a), to do what you want, when you want? This certainly seems like freedom. To me, it conjures up pictures of unspoiled countryside, of being able to walk in the forest, or to settle and build wherever you like and leave doors unlocked at night—but there are probably nearly as many definitions as there are people.

The world is a crowded place. If everyone should attempt to do just what he wanted, the very freedom we seek would inevitably be curtailed by others stepping on our toes.

Perhaps we should select answer (b): to do what you want, as long as it does not interfere with another's freedom. Perhaps this is more like it. If everybody acts as they choose, but with consideration for others, maybe this is freedom.

But the world is a crowded place, and getting more so by the day. In the western states of North America, for example, there were originally no planning or zoning regulations. As people moved in, and the population grew, laws were passed to ensure that the environment was managed in a sensible way. Nowadays it is exceedingly difficult to do what you want when you want in terms of erecting buildings or developing land. Those who live in densely populated European countries have lived with such restrictions for centuries.

As population density goes up, so freedom to do as you like diminishes, finally to be eroded almost altogether. With more and more people, come more and more laws. Cities and towns run successfully only because of the many rules and regulations individuals have to observe within their confines. Planning permission and parking restrictions are normal and, as communities become larger, the need for codes of practice becomes apparent to all. These expressly prevent people from doing just what they want—which would create chaos—and are created for all forms of transport, for public service, advertising, publishing and television, to name but a few. Indeed, road traffic is becoming so congested that the governing bodies of some cities and towns are actively considering banning private cars from their streets. The very reason for owning a car—to go where you want, when you want—is under threat.

Allowing others the freedom to do what they want is easy if they live far away; it is much more difficult if by their very presence they prevent you from fulfilling your own desires.

Today, within limits, physical freedom is impossible. As conditions get more crowded it becomes impossible not to interfere with another's freedom, for the very fact of being alive means that each of us impinges significantly on others. A few, perhaps more sensitive than others, find this difficult to bear and, in their darker moments, believe that they are taking up space and using resources that could be better used by other people. But even the illusory liberation of suicide interferes with the freedom of others. Someone has to clear up the mess, and it is likely that someone will grieve at your passing.

If freedom is not 'doing whatever we want', nor yet 'doing what we want, as long as it does not interfere with others', then the answer must be 'neither of the above', answer (c). So, what is freedom?

When we say we want to be free, what do we mean? Being free certainly has overtones of being able to do what we want, when we want; in practice, however, it usually turns out that we want to be free of the consequences of our actions.

We want to drink and not get a hangover. We want to spend money and never go into the red; to be lazy and yet to amass a fortune; to be safe and secure and still find life exciting; to do nothing and yet have problems solve themselves.

As meditators, we want to neglect to meditate at home and yet make progress on residential courses. We want to be 'caring human beings' and yet never to experience unpleasantness. We want to break the precepts and still develop insight. We want never to guard the senses and yet develop concentration. We want to exert great force in the meditation but become tranquil. We want to avoid systematic mindfulness and yet improve in awareness.

Most of this—as we know in our better moments—is wishful thinking. Even so, many of us are not truly convinced that our own actions are the cause of our difficulties. We refuse to connect what we do with the problems we experience and blame other factors instead.

The drunk with a hangover blames the cheese he ate the night before, or bad beer. The spendthrift blames the credit company for his debt. The lazy man blames the environment for his lack of wealth. Not getting what we want, some of us blame everything but our own behaviour, never considering that we ourselves could be the problem.

On television recently, there was a documentary on the paparazzi, freelance newspaper photographers. One stood out from his fellows. An aggressive man, vitriolic in his hatred of those who obstructed him, it was evident that he never questioned his own actions and responses; he believed unquestioningly that the way he related to others was entirely justified. If people did what he wanted, he was charming. If people obstructed him in any way, he unleashed a vicious, foul-mouthed barrage of hatred against them. It never crossed his mind that he was being unreasonable to expect celebrities and fellow paparazzi always to do exactly what he desired.

While at a superficial level people's difficulties arise from their connections with credit companies or government, meditation exercises or ruthless competitors, that does not mean that those things are the sole or even the prime cause of their problems. The individual's expectations and desires—and his resulting behaviour—have much more to do with his problems than does the world around him. It is probable that he has not considered the price he has to pay for the freedoms he seeks or enjoys. Everything has a price.

Selfish craving always overlooks the true cost of fulfilling desire. Instead of addressing the real problem, we usually unleash our disapproval on something that has nothing to do with it. The drunk gives up eating cheese to avoid a hangover. The spendthrift cuts up his credit cards. The fat person has his stomach stapled. The photographer failing to get a picture verbally abuses his subject. The meditator suffering from tension gives up the meditation exercise.

To find the freedom we seek, things certainly have to change, but they have to change internally rather than externally. It is no good trying to change the world outside—the task would be infinite. The only place that we can start with some assurance of success is with ourselves. We have to take a closer look at our own attitudes and behaviour and entertain the notion, however far-fetched it may seem, that the cause of our lack of freedom lies within ourselves.

* * *

There are several things you can do to ensure your best chance of true freedom. Every one of them rests on the realisation that each of us has to change to conform to the reality of the meditative path, rather than trying to change it to suit ourselves.

The first is to accept that guidelines laid down by the eightfold path and your meditation instructor are necessary to the success of meditation. They are not optional extras. For the meditation to succeed you have to keep the precepts. You have to ensure that your livelihood is right. You have to meditate properly and regularly, and you have to develop your wisdom through study and observation.

It may be necessary to change your job, your lifestyle and your commitments but this is in no way a mandate to abandon those who depend on you; remember that commitment to the welfare of others is an essential foundation of wisdom and compassion.

Second, realise that your personal judgement may not be entirely reliable even if you have been meditating for a long time. Do not abandon the meditation exercise without consulting an instructor. He or she has much more experience than you do—several hours a day, every day, plus a lifestyle dedicated to the teaching. Self-assessment is notoriously difficult.

The third thing you can do to aid progress is to accept things as they are. What we might call proper meditation is to let go your fierce grip on how you think the meditation 'should' be. This, incidentally, applies for all meditators, no matter how tender, no matter how advanced. You need to accept things, including yourself, exactly as they are.

This is how to do it.

For the beginner, instead of refusing to bother with what you think of as trivial and annoying distractions, attend to them all without prejudice. You need a relaxed, repetitive application to the meditation. Acknowledging all the distractions and all the hindrances—including your own doubts, hopes and fears—is a sure way to bring exactly the results you desire, though without seeking them directly.

You need to attend to everything that is going on and never let the mind, as it were, dig itself in, never let it seize implacably on this or that feeling or hindrance or distraction. Just keep it noting, in turn, one after another, all of the things that are happening. Although it seems as though the mind will stay at a superficial level endlessly, after a considerable while it does settle down very happily, very quietly and in just the right way.

For the intermediate meditator, the problem is a little different. Assuming correct application, discomfort nearly always occurs when the meditation is about to move forward into an area of new experience. In fact, the discomfort often heralds real progress. More practice will reveal things never seen before, but only if you let go of ideas of what 'should' be happening.

To allay fears, you can do several things. Have a medical check-up. You laugh, but it will allay the fear that there is something seriously wrong. If the results of the check-up are satisfactory (as they nearly always are), then any discomfort must derive from something that you are doing, or must be due to the meditation itself. To find out which, apply yourself to systematic mindfulness with renewed enthusiasm. If you are doing it to yourself, you will soon find out.

Do more practice, not less. Remember that the meditation is supposed to show the nature of *dukkha*, suffering, unsatisfactoriness, discomfort, frustration and so forth, so it is no wonder that there are stages within the practice where these things are accentuated.

The most effective thing you can do is simply to accept the pain, the nausea, the discomfort, and refuse to give in. You will find it astonishing what a difference such decision and determination can make. Remember that at the beginning of your instruction in meditation you were told to sit still. If you do this then many of the minor irritations disappear. If, in contrast, you constantly try to shift limbs and body to find a better, less painful position, that can go on for hour after hour without finding any lasting relief.

The established meditator also has to let go. Even when you have developed deep mindfulness and concentration you still have to let go, but now you have to let go of control and, to a lesser extent, clarity. When successful, there is pure observation of the flow of life, internally and externally. This is the sphere of true learning; this is where the work is done; this is where insight is born. Letting go of control with mindfulness and concentration well established allows everything to come and go in its own time, not as you dictate.

When there is no 'steering' of the meditation, all mental and physical states, including occasional hindrances, arise and pass away quickly. Sounds, feelings, thoughts—everything—come and go and, because you have given up controlling the practice, at this level they can be observed to arise and fall away almost instantaneously.

You begin then to realise that things seem to stay in existence only because we grasp at them. We reach out and cling to this or that thing that we love or hate, for there is just as much clinging associated with hatred as there is with the craving that some call love. True love, incidentally, has no clinging, no grasping, for it desires only what is best for the other.

In the absence of clinging, with the mind balanced, repeated practice reveals every facet of human nature and shows that they all arise and pass away in less time than it takes to tell. Insight arises that transience does not mean that things 'change' but that they are truly impermanent: everything arises only to die almost at once. It is a salutary experience.

For all meditators, accepting things as they are is a question of being prepared to let go, to leap into the unknown. In many cases, the unknown is merely something that you have never had the patience to try before. It might be to include in your observation all the distractions you normally ignore when you meditate and being prepared to do nothing but that. Whatever your personal 'unknown', preparing to leap into it is like hanging by your hands from the edge of a precipice in the dark. You have no idea whether the ground is just under your feet or a fatal drop below. There is only one certain way to find out, and that is to let go.

The only freedom lies in acceptance. True acceptance—not resignation—means that you approach things in a way never tried before. Instead of trying always to adjust the environment, or yourself, or always tweaking the meditation to get it going this way or that, now you simply observe what takes place, internally and externally, without any interference whatsoever.

This new attitude of acceptance brings other changes in outlook. At the gross level, the outer level, you come to have far less personal interest in things like politics and power struggles, conservation and the state of the world. While these things are vitally important, you understand now that each of us is in fact responsible for what he is and for his own position in life. You certainly do all you can for others but at the same time keep the goal in sight. The aim of applying the Buddha's teachings is to have a mind entirely free from all traces of craving, hatred and attachment, for it is these—and not politics or pollution—that are the true causes of suffering in the world.

Inwardly, acceptance means that you see and accept the facts of your own nature—both good and bad parts of it—without self-hatred and without self-blame. You have come to love your personal internal enemies and have compassion for them.

You do not turn into a robot, as some fear—far from it: life is far more rewarding, fulfilling, exciting and mysterious. You open yourself to reality, never knowing what is coming next, but secure in the knowledge and understanding that the universe is benevolent; that everything that happens is fundamentally in our own interests. You are ever vulnerable but always safe.

You are then free from believing that anything in the world could be a final answer to suffering: not pleasant feeling, not concentration, not even insight, for you see that craving and clinging are the culprits. Eventually, these vanish in the light of wisdom, never more to return. There is then total freedom from psychological dependence on anything whatsoever. You are forever free and life is perfect as it is.

4

Rites of Passage

Rites of passage are rituals that mark the transition from one state of being to another, typically from youth to adulthood. Often purely ceremonial, as in presenting a young person with a symbolic key to the front door of the house, the rituals can be true ordeals that are extremely challenging, even life-threatening. In some cases, they are considered so important to the community that specific individuals are appointed custodians to maintain the rites and assess the success of the candidates.

Our own culture seems at first glance to have lost its rites of passage—an eighteenth birthday party does not somehow seem significant enough to qualify. Closer examination, though, reveals similar practices in many walks of life. Ask any apprentice, ask any newly appointed manager, ask the newcomer to almost any group of people who work together, and he will usually tell of an 'initiation' into his new circle. Indeed, we all suffer trials as we grow into adulthood and beyond. In one sense, our entire life is a series of tests, a series of opportunities to learn lessons that, if successful, help us to grow in understanding and maturity.

Rites of passage, formal or not, are important milestones on the path of self-knowledge and self-development. Nowhere is this truer than the spiritual path. We have to undergo definite trials in our transition from the mundane to the spiritual. The ordeals are very real, though they may appear to the candidate in mythological or symbolic form. For instance, on the Toltec path that the Yaqui Indian, Don Juan Matus, taught Carlos Castaneda, one of the 'guardians' of that path that Carlos had to pass appeared to him as a gnat of terrifying proportions.

The symbols or myths represent an underlying truth, for the guardians of the true spiritual path are real. Though the path seems so readily available today, with written material easily to hand and many who teach, on closer examination that turns out not to be the case. Entry into the true way is gained only by the successful completion of formidable rites of passage. In this talk, I want to look at the teaching of the Buddha to see how this works, though much of what follows applies equally to many spiritual paths in existence today.

* * *

Thanks to the tireless efforts of translators, historians and adventurous scholars who have travelled the far-off corners of the world in search of truth, the teachings of the Buddha are available across the world in just about every widely used language. In the West, the Buddha's teaching is potentially plain for all to see. You can buy a book, take a university course or study with a Dhamma teacher, ordained or lay. All the details you could possibly wish for—historical, philosophical, cultural—all are there for the taking.

You can study *Sutta* (the discourses), *Vinaya* (the rules and discipline) and *Abhidhamma* (the higher philosophical teaching), to any extent and to great depths, and do all of this with easy access to nearly all levels of this pristine teaching. With work, you can become an expert in those subjects, as well as in historical philology, in Pali, Sanskrit, Tibetan, Burmese, Thai or Chinese, and even in the historical development of different sects and their different teachings—and still you will know nothing of the spiritual path.

To know anything of the spiritual path you have to *practise* what the Buddha taught. You have physically and mentally to train in a spiritual discipline that will begin to wear away the veils that hide the infinite. But even practice of a spiritual way is not on its own enough to ensure entry to the true and secret path. The true path is hidden in ways hard for many of us to understand. It hides in plain sight, as it were, and is all the more difficult to find for that.

In India, home of spirituality, years ago I met many Westerners on the search for truth. They were a mixed lot: young and old, determined and lost, hard-headedly sane, and some without question several cards short of a full deck. I met or heard of seekers who had wandered throughout the varied countries of the East. Some had sought wise men in Africa or among the peoples of the South Seas.

All of them were sincere but, looking back, it is doubtful if more than one or perhaps two of those I met really knew what they were doing. Many of the rest were lost. Much later on my teacher was to call them 'wanderers in a wasteland', a term he used also for those poor individuals who, lost in the universes of lysergic acid or heroin, used occasionally to call at the door of the monastery seeking help. The drugs of choice may be different today, but the problem is much the same.

The secret of the true path is heavily guarded. While teachings are available to all who ask, conditions of entry to the secret path are stringent in the extreme. It is not enough simply to search—there has to be sacrifice. There are challenging ordeals to go through. Calling yourself a Buddhist will not do it. Study is not enough. Practice can be nothing more than simulation, mimicry, acting. There has to be internal revolution, and that comes only at a price.

We can divide the ordeals or trials we have to face into two kinds: physical and mental. The physical ordeals are all a matter of self-restraint. They demand a brake on runaway desires; they constrain our behaviour as far as the external world is concerned. It is always possible, though not necessarily comfortable, to comply with their demands, however much we might secretly like to do otherwise.

The mental tests are of a different order, for success is impossible to imitate convincingly. While most of us do try imitation at first, the custodians of the secret path cannot be bribed, cajoled or fooled. The secret ingredient—among the many necessary qualities that ensure success—seems to be faith that there is something beyond, that there is indeed an answer.

★ ★ ★

How can one succeed when seeking entry to the true path? What does it take to satisfy the guardians, to win through the ordeals, to pass the tests? What are the greatest obstacles, and how may they be overcome?

In general terms, given at least basic right views that we will look at later, the overriding barrier to progress is excessive self-concern, conceit. Wherever 'self' is stressed over the welfare of others, there is at that time an insuperable hurdle and this is right away to fail the test, to fall foul of the guardian, to miss one's aim at the spiritual path. The one quality that seems to offset this kind of conceit is faith arising out of suffering. This is not blind belief in creed or doctrine, but rather the unrelenting and intense conviction that there must be an answer to the problem of suffering, to the questions of life and death. Faith allows the possibility of easier self-sacrifice, of easier abandonment of selfish advantage. It is the key to the door to freedom.

The physical obstacles are the trials posed by the familiar five precepts. Trying to keep these fully and honestly diminishes self-concern. If we seek to overcome these obstacles through the exercise of great and anxious self-interest, however, we make little or no progress, for self-concern grows rather than diminishes. Success demands the restraint of self-interest. Let us look briefly at the precepts to see how they work.

The five are: I undertake the rule of training to refrain from …

  … killing or harming living creatures.
  … taking what is not given.
  … all unlawful sexual intercourse.
  … lying, slander, gossip, tale-bearing, backbiting and all forms of
      harsh or frivolous speech.
  … intoxicating drinks and substances.

To avoid onslaught on creatures would seem to be easy enough. But how far do you take it? Note that here we are talking about only those actions performed by our own hands or that someone else performs at our express command. How far do you go? Do you commission the vet to kill the family pet when it is on its way out? Do you kill ants, woodlice, spiders and mice that sometimes invade the family home? Where do you draw the line? If you have a problem with ant infestation, as we did recently, why not try asking the ants kindly to leave? You may be surprised at the result. There is rarely any need for violence.

Refraining from taking what is not given includes stealing but is broader than an injunction against theft alone, for this precept enjoins consideration of others to a much more subtle degree. It needs sensitivity to the feelings of those around you and recognition of what you, personally, find offensive. If you understand that others may be similarly upset, restraint is very much easier.

You could interpret 'refraining from unlawful sexual intercourse' as not taking liberties, for any sensual behaviour that is blameable by most others is what is intended. While this precept usually applies to sexual behaviour, it is worth remembering that sensual desires cover a very broad field indeed. The Buddha stated, on more than one occasion, that sensual desires were responsible for all the ills of the world, from minor personal disagreements to international wars. People can get extremely angry about something as relatively trivial as finding towels 'reserving' sun-beds for later use.

The tongue is a formidable weapon and can bring extreme discord to a previously harmonious group or even to the wider community. Restraint of harmful speech patterns is difficult, for people love to gossip and many use harsh language without thinking. Harmful speech is also upsetting to the mind of the person who practises it as, to a lesser extent, is constant frivolity. Wrong speech has to be reined in if progress is desired.

For those intent upon the spiritual path, intoxication is counter-productive. The development of insight leading to emergence from *samsāra*, the round of suffering, rests upon mindful attention and clear comprehension. Both of these are rendered impossible by intoxication whether induced by alcohol or drugs, 'soft' or otherwise. Some argue that certain drugs allow glimpses of states of mind beyond the normal. While this can apply under certain circumstances, usually the individual has no training to comprehend or use drug-induced states of mind, however 'exalted', far less the training to replicate them at will; indeed, if he had the training, he would not need the drugs.

To summarise the physical ordeals: all physical restraint is easily possible with some effort. Physical restraint may be done for selfish reasons, and even for great self-aggrandisement. I have heard somebody say, '*I* keep the precepts perfectly, but I know *you* do not!' An individual can still harbour much mental inefficiency, even while acting impeccably, for we do not need to bring the mind fully into play to overcome the physical ordeals.

The mental conditions for entry to the secret path, the true path, are by far the hardest to fulfil. They are tests of inner attitudes and motivations concerning both worldly and 'spiritual' matters and, as such, bear on all aspects of our mental behaviour. Some people pretend to have completed the mental trials successfully, to have passed the tests but, generally, they fool only themselves. The signs of self-deceit or imitation are obvious to those who know; they stand out like the smell downwind of a sewage-works in high summer.

What are the mental conditions that need to be met? They are these: the student must be not covetous, not malevolent in mind and not of wrong view. I want to look in more detail at what it means to satisfy each of these requirements.

In each case, it is possible to put on a face, to pretend that one is 'holy' or 'spiritual'. I am sure we have all met those sickly sweet or arrogantly remote individuals who claim to be practising a religious way. You know the ones I mean—the ones you know are too good to be true and who provoke in you the urge to batter them until they reveal their true feelings. Such pretenders to the crown of spiritual progress will never pass the tests until they change internally. This rite of passage is successful only when there is genuine abandonment of the obstacles. We can never succeed by wishful thinking or play-acting. In every case, success is founded on a blend of faith and wisdom, as we shall see.

The student is not covetous. He experiences genuine fellow-feeling for others and does not envy their good fortune, recognising that material and mental gains come only from hard work and generosity in the past. The student accepts that the actions we perform are our own responsibility, that his lot in this life overall and at this particular time is as it is because of what he has done in the past. He sees that it could not be any other way and that this rule is valid for everyone. There is with this attitude the implicit recognition of the law of *kamma*, of action and result and, by extension, recognition or acceptance of rebirth from life to life. The student recognises that actions performed with craving and attachment produce suffering, that yearning for things belonging to another is a pointless exercise that can only produce grief. He or she firmly believes that peace of mind is immeasurably more valuable than anything another person may possess.

The student is not malevolent in mind. He or she assumes or has discovered that the universe is essentially benevolent, in spite of all the seemingly contradictory evidence. The student prefers to preserve life and recognises that to damage others is also to damage oneself.

The implications of this law of action are far-reaching. For instance, any action will have its results in the life-stream of the one who performs it, selfish actions producing disaster, unselfish actions producing happiness. Those foolish or evil individuals who have harmed others will surely reap the results of their actions in misery and self-loathing, not to mention the possibility of a less fortunate rebirth. There is no need for a victim to act to 'get even'. Rather than seeking revenge, it would be far more appropriate to feel compassion for the wrongdoer than to wish to harm him or her in turn, thereby to bring about one's own future distress.

The student is not of wrong view. Being 'not of wrong view' actually includes much of what we have covered so far. For clarity, though, it is useful to deal with this under a separate heading. It covers at least an outline understanding of the following points: the five aspects of mundane right view, the four noble truths and last, but not least, faith in the Buddha, the Dhamma and the Sangha—the group of men and women who have discovered the truth through the teaching of the Buddha, or their equivalents on other paths.

The five points of mundane right view:

Actions have results.
There is result of giving.
There are mother and father.
There are spontaneously arisen beings.
There are teachers who know this world and the world beyond.

We have already looked briefly at the fact that actions have results.

The second mundane right view is that there is result of giving. Generosity (whether in respect of goods, money, time or consideration) is always rewarded personally. If you wish to be rich, give a lot away. If you want to be happy, give your time and efforts in the service of others. There is result of giving.

'There are mother and father.' We owe a great debt of gratitude to parents for having brought us into the human realm, reared us and given us the chance of life here. It is only in the human realm that beings have a good chance of establishing themselves on the spiritual path, because here there is a roughly even balance between pleasure and pain, between good and bad.

The fourth right view is that there are 'spontaneously arisen beings'. There are realms other than the human, normally invisible to human sight, where there exist conscious beings. These beings arise 'spontaneously'—which means they are 'born' without the need for parents, much as is the body we use in dreams. It may well be that, dying from the human realm, we ourselves become spontaneously arisen on a level other than human.

Lastly, there are teachers who know and teach these things.

For happiness in the world, these five mundane right views form an indispensable foundation. Without at least some of them there is no ethical basis for behaviour and licence is likely to predominate, bringing anguish to all who get embroiled in it. Self-serving behaviour always becomes a downward spiral of indulgence, grasping and distress. Restraint, conditioned by the five mundane right views, can be personally proven to bring a reduction of mental and emotional pain, as well as a reduction in physical danger.

Ethical behaviour is the bedrock of successful community living. It is also the foundation of whatever happiness is possible in the world for the individual. However, no matter how refined it becomes, ethical behaviour cannot eradicate distress. For that, we need to turn to the heart of the Buddha's teaching, the four noble truths.

There exists suffering. The existence of suffering seems hardly deniable but many a person who comes to this way says, 'Of course, I do not really suffer, I do not have any problems, I am just interested in meditation.' I think that what they mean is that there is no evidence of gross distress in their lives; there is no illness, no grief, no broken relationship, no depression. Initially unaware of the many subtle areas of distress, with more insight they usually realise that they do experience considerable unease and dissatisfaction. Indeed, I suggest that no one would seek to put himself through meditative training unless he was aware at the very least of a certain lack in his life. That sense of something lacking *is* suffering.

There exists a cause of suffering. Suffering does not arise randomly or fortuitously but on definite conditions that can be known and understood. The major cause or condition on which suffering arises is craving and the attachment to which it leads.

There exists the cessation of suffering. All suffering can completely cease by eradicating the very conditions upon which it depends. The end of suffering is not a myth or a theory; it is a fact that anyone can, with the right sort of work, prove for themselves, because ...

There exists a way leading to the cessation of suffering. There is a clearly defined, effective and current path that will take anyone who follows it faithfully to the cessation of suffering. We know it today as the Buddha's eightfold path. It can be divided into three areas of personal endeavour: restraint of physical actions through the practice of ethical behaviour; development of the capacity to pay concentrated attention to mental and physical states; development of the meditative insight that will lead to knowledge of bliss and freedom from suffering.

We also need faith. We need faith in the Buddha—faith that he did exist, that he was enlightened, that he did know the way. We need faith in the Dhamma, his teaching—that it is valid, that it was valid then and it is still valid today, that it does work. We need faith in the Sangha, those meditators who have come to know the truth through the teaching of the Buddha. They exist today both in and out of the monastic Order and now, at this very time, some of these living people can teach us the way to the end of suffering.

With one-pointed efforts to apply the teaching of the Buddha, this kind of generalised faith gradually becomes total confidence in what he taught, for we see through our own experience that it works. This is a long way from blind faith, for it is based on much personal experience as well as ever-increasing understanding of the way distress arises and ceases.

* * *

It sometimes happens that a student of the mysteries is temporarily unable to learn from his human teachers and cannot complete the rites of passage to the true path. Confusion may be the problem: a student, though sincere, may be so vague and confused as to be unable to follow instruction. Or perhaps the student sets himself above his teachers, with an implacable conceit that nothing seems able to dent.

This conceit has two variants. The first is, 'I am going to do it my way, whatever you say or do. I will just use your facilities to make things easier for me and ignore what you have to say.' The second variant is, 'My particular case is so extraordinary, so special, that I doubt whether anyone can help me. I will take instruction from you, but I do not really expect that you have—or anyone has, for that matter—the skill to help me overcome my special difficulties. I really do stand apart from the rest of humanity. There is no one who could possibly know just how much I suffer.'

When this happens, when someone consistently and wilfully refuses to tackle the tests that are the entrance examination to the true path, there is one great teacher to whom such an intractable case is assigned. The greatest teacher in the world is the law of *kamma*. If someone consistently chooses the wrong path, that law ensures continued and increasing suffering that repeats and repeats until, driven to desperation, the individual reaches out to others and starts to learn the lessons he needs to understand.

Incidentally, if you suspect that you may qualify to be taught in this way, you can gain more evidence by looking back through the things you count as failures. Is there a pattern? Is it always 'the circumstances' that prevent you from succeeding? Is it other people? Does no one ever realise just how difficult your personal circumstances are? Are employers, colleagues and friends always inconsiderate of your special problems? Do the same kinds of difficulties keep recurring? If you answer 'yes' to any of these, you have lessons to learn. One way to start learning is to entertain the possibility, however remote, that the fault might be yours alone.

* * *

To learn about the spiritual path, we can buy books, take a university course or study with a Dhamma teacher. All the details we could possibly wish for—historical, philological, philosophical or cultural—are there for the taking. We can study the books to any extent and to great depths. We can become experts in every aspect of the Buddha's teaching. But we will know nothing of the spiritual path without practice, without faith, without the right attitude.

To succeed in our rites of passage to the true path, the real path, we have to satisfy the guardians of that path; we have to pass certain tests and ordeals. We cannot pretend to have passed them; we have actually to do so.

If we wish to progress, we have no option but to change. How do we change? We change through experience, through living life in all its intensity and by observing what happens. This process cannot be accomplished successfully without the systematic development of mindfulness and concentration. We need also to study the words of wise men. We need great self-restraint and much courage to face our own shortcomings. But even all this is not enough; we have also to learn the path of love.

Progress beyond a certain point is impossible unless we overcome malevolence of mind. We have to cease fearing our neighbours or envying their successes. We have to become a joyful part of all life without always looking elsewhere for our satisfaction. In short, we need mundane wisdom, won by direct and sensitive experience of living in the real world, and supramundane insight, won through taking up the burden of the meditation on transience. For this, we need a teacher skilled in the ways of meditation. Together these bring us the intelligence to know how to think and act, and the wisdom to stop thinking and acting against our own and others' best interests.

There is not one rite of passage but many, and they take many forms. Each new challenge is a test of our wisdom or compassion. Whether we pass or fail, win or lose, the choice is entirely our own, however much we may protest to the contrary. Follow faithfully the path of the Buddha, though, and life becomes incomparably easier, for the teaching is a route-map to the infinite where suffering of any description cannot exist.

In the end, we realise that no one can do it for us. Teachers can but point the way; the effort to walk the path is our responsibility alone.

Success is possible, today, just as it was when the Buddha was alive. We can overcome all the trials, pass all the tests, defeat all the obstacles. Each of us can, with work, become 'one of the great ones, with burden laid down', one of the 'true men' (and women) of whom the Buddha spoke so often. It is not an idle dream. Far from it! The path exists. Teachers exist. The opportunity exists. All that remains is the effort.

5

Getting the Most Out of Life

Everywhere you look, there are people. No two of us are completely alike. Each of us is distinguishable from his fellows, not only through physical characteristics, but also through personality, character, emotional make-up, interests and state of happiness—some are happy, some are miserable.

Why are we so different? The short answer is *kamma* and *vipāka*, action and resultant. We create our own lives internally and externally by the ways in which we choose to act. If we act unskilfully, selfishly, then suffering follows us inexorably. If on the other hand we choose to act with a view to non-harming, wisely, unselfishly, then we experience beauty and pleasure even to the end of our days. Countless different past lives have conditioned the present life in countless different ways. Our lives are different; our reactions to events are different. We are different.

For example, how do *you* handle failure and disappointment? Do you accept it, shrug your shoulders and move on—or do you assume that you can probably overcome the failure if you try hard enough? Perhaps, instead, you blame the external world for the difficulty, or get angry with other people when they 'cross' you. Perhaps you get angry at any setback. Some do: some rage at traffic lights when they turn to red in their path; some get furious when it rains, or when it is too hot or too cold. People are different; they respond differently to events that are apparently the same.

* * *

All of us are a mixture of dark and light qualities. Light is our noble side; it is the presence of ennobling qualities like faith, intelligence and wisdom, and choosing to guide our lives by adherence to ethical or spiritual values. Dark is the harmful side of our nature; it is ignorance, craving, hatred and contempt for ethical or spiritual values.

Light and dark can also represent the outcome of skilful and unskilful actions. The Buddha said there were four kinds of people. There were those born in the dark and heading for the dark; those born in the dark but heading for the light; those born in the light and heading for the dark; and, of course, those born in the light and heading for the light.

Someone born in the dark is born into distressed circumstances. These could be poverty, war or famine; they could be homelessness, disease, or physical or mental disability. Someone born in the light is born into favoured or privileged circumstances; surrounded by relative wealth and comfort, he or she has access to many avenues of education and self-expression.

The circumstances of birth are most definitely not the deciding factor in the choices we make. Environmental factors certainly condition our actions, but they do not provide the necessary condition for them. In other words, we do have a real choice; whether born in the light or the dark, we can choose to act wisely or unwisely. If we habitually use greed, violence and coercion to get what we want, we are heading for the dark no matter where we were born—and our next rebirth is likely to be considerably worse than this one. If we choose, instead, to lead an ethical life, with the accent on non-harming, on faith and spiritual values, we will be reborn into the light, into circumstances more pleasant than this life—irrespective of the circumstances of birth in this lifetime.

It is never easy to select a course of action from the tangle of opportunities that face us. If down and out, is it ethically acceptable to steal to support yourself, rather than being a drain on the state by accepting social security payments? When drawing unemployment benefit, is it ethically acceptable to work without notifying the authorities? Trying to pay off a crippling mortgage, is it ethically acceptable to overestimate your expenses by a factor of two hundred percent, given that you and your family might be homeless otherwise? How do you decide where to draw the line?

We have to ask what we want out of life. What are we trying to achieve? Simplifying greatly, we can say that we all have one of three distinct objectives, and this greatly affects the way we respond to events. Each of us wants to gain a physical, a mental/emotional or a spiritual advantage from the actions we perform.

If we want physical fulfilment, we seek sensual ease, relaxation and physical stimulation. If we want mental or emotional fulfilment, we seek mental development through education, for instance, or emotional experience through relationships or artistic endeavours. Those seeking spiritual fulfilment want peace of mind, including freedom from mental ills such as guilt and loneliness; they want to ensure a profitable rebirth or, ultimately, to eliminate all dissatisfaction whatsoever.

★ ★ ★

People are very different. They approach all aspects of daily living differently, and this can have a profound bearing on how they choose to get the best out of life. Someone seeking fulfilment at the physical level, for example, is going to respond to circumstances very differently from someone whose major concern is for spiritual advantage. A further conditioning factor is whether the individual is heading for the light or the dark; the strong ethical standard of someone heading for the light will set his course apart from one heading for the dark.

Let us look at the options open to the various individuals, starting with someone whose highest priority is physical fulfilment. His ideals can range from sensual indulgence and constant stimulation at one end of the spectrum to sensory restraint, relaxation and moderation at the other.

Those heading for the dark attempt to satisfy bodily desires selfishly through any means available. Trying to get their own way right now, this instant, they rarely consider others' welfare in their attempts to achieve their pleasures.

In contrast, those heading for the light prefer to seek physical satisfaction through moderation and hard work and tend to favour positive and mild-mannered interaction with others rather than confrontation.

Seeking mental or emotional fulfilment is more complex. It can involve seeking one's own emotional advantage in ways that harm others and can include every aspect of seeking satisfaction through material means. It can involve developing positive mental skills. In the best cases, it includes attempts to establish a sense of contentment and freedom from guilt by developing consideration for others.

Heading for the dark, we attempt to gain mental satisfaction unwisely by, for example, seeking status or power over others by using questionable means. We bully and persecute, nag and criticise, or spread defamatory rumours. Some even turn to black magic to gain an emotional hold over others, thus to make themselves feel secure. We may seek to protect ourselves emotionally by defensiveness, secretiveness, being afraid of any human interaction in case it upsets our fragile personal balance. In the worst cases, criticism becomes persecution and the kind of intolerance that leads to the horrors of so called 'ethnic cleansing'. All because we desire to feel safe and free from threat.

Those heading for the light believe that personal fulfilment cannot be attained through harming other beings. Instead, they practise consideration of others' feelings and try always to be tolerant and even-handed. Rather than cheat or bully their way up the ladder of success, those heading for the light choose to work, perhaps to develop mental skills to increase their opportunities in the world. They emphasise a balanced lifestyle, always conscious that moderation is a good thing. Often practising members of a religion, many have found that religious belief and ritual can provide great emotional support.

When looking at ways in which we seek spiritual advantage, there seem at first to be a great number. In brief, however, to seek spiritual advantage is to aim to establish and maintain peace of mind; to ensure a profitable rebirth, whether in a heaven or in the next life as a human being; and ultimately to eliminate dissatisfaction. This final goal is usually seen either as union with an all-powerful being or as becoming enlightened, depending upon your point of view.

Those heading for the dark may seek their spiritual advantage through persecution of others in the name of a religion or a similar belief system. Such oppression can range from extreme holier-than-thou attitudes, through over-zealous missionary work, to overt physical 'persuasion', always in the name of the good and the true. One obvious example is the extracting of 'confessions' during the Spanish Inquisition.

Those heading for the light seek their spiritual advantage through things like service, renunciation and sense-restraint. If knowledgeable, they will practise the *parami* (the perfections) and the *Brahma-vihāra* (the 'divine abidings') in whatever form they know of them, as well as probably practising recollections to encourage the mind in these activities. Ultimately, the one way to ensure spiritual advantage is to practise *samatha* and *vipassanā* meditations, concentration and insight meditations, more of which in a moment.

★ ★ ★

The Buddha explained all of this in detail. He laid down a teaching that cuts through the jungle of views and possibilities and provides us with a clear and unequivocal message. Our personal advantage at any level is best served by following the right eightfold path. Explanation of the eight factors includes instructions for dealing with all our actions and reactions—physical, verbal and mental. Following these guidelines, we will never lose our way. We will always aim at our own highest happiness, and will be, at the very least, harmless to those around us and, at the best, of great assistance to them in their search for satisfaction and peace of mind.

To remind you, let us take a brief look at the eight factors.

The first is **right view** or right understanding that, essentially, is knowledge of the four noble truths. Right view is right understanding of these truths from the elementary level where it can be expressed by, 'There must be more than this', to full gnosis at the very end of the path to freedom.

Right thought is thought and aspiration free from craving, free from hatred, free from attachment. It is, therefore, the renunciation of attachment and selfishness in terms of restraint, and the practice of loving-kindness and compassion when developing positive qualities of mind.

Right speech is refraining from falsehood, slander, harsh speech and frivolous talk.

Right action is refraining from killing, from stealing and from sexual misconduct.

Right livelihood is essentially to avoid occupations that encourage killing or harming other beings. The books go into some detail and give specific trades that one should avoid. They include trading in arms; trading in human beings (slavery); trading in flesh, or breeding animals for slaughter; dealing in intoxicating drinks and poisons for the purpose of killing living things.

Right effort consists of four components: the effort to overcome unwholesome states; the effort to prevent them arising in future; the effort to encourage positive states; and the effort to maintain them once they are established.

The last of the four right efforts is often the most difficult to accomplish. Frequently, meditators find that successful suppression of the hindrances is followed by some difficulties. Once the mind has become very still and peaceful, rather than accepting it and trying to maintain the calm, many meditators' first reaction is 'What next?' This response immediately re-introduces imbalance and disturbance. Trying to maintain a positive state that has arisen is a skill that needs cultivation.

Following right effort is **right mindfulness**, and this is to be constantly setting up mindfulness—ideally, mindfulness of transience—on the right objects. Briefly, the right objects for mindfulness, for discriminative awareness, are body, feelings, states of mind and content of mind.

Finally, there is **right concentration**. Right concentration is learning how to focus the mind, learning how to make it one-pointed. If all distractions can be eliminated temporarily, then great tranquillity can result and many internal processes become much more apparent. Concentration, one-pointed attention, aids penetration through the murk so that you can see the truth of things as they are.

Right effort, right mindfulness and right concentration together are meditation, the very heart of the Buddha's path to lasting peace of mind. Meditation is supported by the calmness of mind developed by the personal restraint described in right speech, right action and right livelihood. Right view and right aspiration direct one's efforts to overcome suffering completely.

The eightfold path is a true guide. Guiding one's life by these right principles, personal advantage is assured. It demands personal restraint; it demands restraint of selfish indulgence and selfish activity; it demands work and perseverance. But, given those things, anyone can prove that this method of development does what it claims. It is often called 'the way to heaven' and, followed faithfully, it is just that. It is the certain path to a rebirth in the light, whether as human or higher.

It is less well-known that the Buddha also outlined a wrong eightfold path. Instead of right view and right thought, it starts with wrong view and wrong thought. It covers wrong action of all kinds—physical, verbal and mental. All aspects of that wrong path predispose an individual towards greater and greater suffering. Following the wrong path, one is inexorably destined for the dark—unless, of course, one changes.

To follow the right path we have deliberately to turn away from the wrong one. We have to let go of the unskilful. Letting go, turning towards the light, the sun rises on the pathway to paradise. Following the path of the Buddha, you do not need to worry if you are doing the best for yourself. Hundreds and thousands of people could tell you for a fact that you are but even that does not matter, for you can find out for yourself that it is true. Follow the path conscientiously for five years and you will never look back. Let alone five years, two years is entirely enough to prove its worth. Even two months can change your outlook entirely, can change it for the better and irrevocably. The eightfold path is all you will ever need to get the most out of life.

6

The Six Impossibilities

After four days on a massive cruise ship, the travel-programme presenter was breathlessly describing the experience. The two thousand passengers, and their crew, could have everything they wanted. She told us that the ship's extensive kitchens supplied *eight* formal meals a day and that, should you feel deprived between them, there were many opportunities for snacks. If snacks were not enough, one of the several bars could distract you for a while or, if sedentary drinking palled, a number of discos provided music and dancing. For those who preferred a cultural bias to their sensual enjoyment, three theatres provided a wide selection of shows. Sporty passengers were not forgotten: there were two swimming pools and endless deck games. Obviously impressed, the presenter described it as, 'Fun, fun, fun all the way!'

Advertisements and television programmes urge us to take increasingly expensive holidays and to indulge ourselves in entertainment of all descriptions. They bombard us with exhortations to purchase anything and everything, including cheap loans to pay for it all. It will be worthwhile, we are told, because we will look younger, be fitter, sexier, live longer, be richer. We are encouraged, even ordered, to have a good time, to enjoy ourselves, to make of life one long party.

We are being sold a fantasy, a picture that cannot possibly live up to the realities of normal existence. Even if we believe we are mature enough to discount the propaganda, when faced with the reality of the daily round we are often quite unprepared to cope, not least because of the distorted images we have absorbed through the all-pervasive media. Some of the things we are persuaded to buy are actively harmful to health and the environment; others are not remotely necessary for a happy life. The rosy picture painted by advertising is difficult to align with the true state of affairs, which is often depressing and unwelcome. We do not like to see things like increasing traffic congestion, used-car graveyards, landfill sites, drug abuse, greed, crime and fraud.

The sheer slog of keeping going drives some of us to distraction. Commuter stress, job insecurity, work pressure, ageing and illness all contradict the alluring propaganda we are fed every day. Nowhere is this more apparent than when confronted with death. When it threatens someone close, in 'real life', the very prospect of death—let alone the sight of it—is terrifying to entirely too many of us. The experience has an awful immediacy completely missing from the newspapers, radio or television.

Thinking about it, we begin to realise that there has to be another way. Grasping after a dream cannot be the way to find happiness and satisfaction.

While adequate food, shelter and healthcare are essential for basic existence, happiness is different. We do not *need* happiness to live, though life is much more fulfilling if we are happy and contented. Further, happiness is not dependent on health, wealth or a full stomach. Happiness in the world certainly does not depend upon going on holiday or being dressed in the latest fashion. It is not founded upon eating out twice a week or buying a new stereo. Real happiness is a far subtler affair and comes from reducing craving, not encouraging it. Real happiness is a matter of reducing and finally eliminating the craving that grasps first at this, then at that, in the belief that it will bring the happiness we seek.

The Buddha, who re-discovered this principle over 2,500 years ago, summarised his teaching in the four noble truths. The fourth truth, the way leading to the end of suffering, is a means of bringing one's life into line with the reality of existence. It can be summed up by a verse found in the *Dhammapada*: 'Cease to do evil; cultivate the good; purify the mind. This is the teaching of all Buddhas.'

The Buddha spent forty-five years teaching others the details of how to put this advice into practice. His teachings are recorded in the Pali Canon, a huge collection of works covering every aspect of the search for happiness.

We 'cease to do evil' by keeping the five precepts. We 'cultivate the good' by practising and making much of the four *Brahma-vihāra*, the four 'divine abidings'. We purify the mind by practising *vipassanā*, eventually attaining to complete freedom, *nibbāna*, the deathless, that which has been called the highest happiness and which the Buddha identified as the complete cessation of suffering.

The foundation of the entire eightfold path is personal restraint of what the verse calls evil, of the selfish, grasping activity that rides roughshod over other people. Restraint of selfish grasping is the foundation for internal and external harmony and no one can successfully walk the spiritual path without it. But simply refraining from selfish physical activity is not enough, for the mind may remain violent and greedy. One has also to cultivate the good.

When I was in training, one of my duties was to answer the door to people who called at the monastery. The callers were often people who would best be described as hippies—they certainly had long hair, wore beads and sometimes a flower behind the ear. Many of them came to preach love and kindness and were, I think, quite genuine in their wish for a better life for everyone. It was most noticeable, however, that in many cases they radiated a fierce hatred and agitation of which they seemed quite unaware. It was evident that they had not actually cultivated love but had instead attempted to crush down all hatred and negative aspects of mind. They had crushed them down with such a fierce hand that the 'evil' was festering beneath the surface. They had not actually cultivated the good but had merely 'papered over the cracks' with a display of love and peace that was less than convincing because of its shaky foundations.

There is no finer way to 'cultivate the good' than to practise the meditations called the divine abidings (*Brahma-vihāra*). They are loving-kindness, compassion, sympathetic joy and equanimity. Each of these temporarily negates all vicious and harmful states of mind and, as such, offers eleven traditional benefits.

Practising loving-kindness, say, to good effect, a meditator can expect to sleep in comfort; can expect to wake happily; can expect never to have a nightmare. He or she will be dear to human beings, being liked by everyone, and will be dear to non-human beings, including animals and celestial devas whom we are not able ordinarily to see. Someone who has made much of such meditations will be guarded by those very deities who will look out for his or her welfare. Danger in the form of weapons, fire and poison does not afflict the person who is skilled in this mode of meditation. The mind is easily concentrated and that calmness and serenity shows itself in a bright and serene countenance. Finally, if they do not make it all the way to enlightenment, they are certain to be reborn in one of the more pleasant worlds.

All eleven benefits are derived from practising any of the divine abidings, each of which counteracts a specific negative quality or tendency. Loving-kindness counteracts hatred. Compassion counteracts cruelty. Sympathetic joy counteracts avarice. Equanimity counteracts passion. Before practising one of these meditations to overcome a specific negative quality, however, it is wise to get some idea of the problems with which you are faced.

Initially, some people are unaware of even the approximate make-up of their minds, let alone whether they experience habitual mental states of hatred or avarice. There are several ways to find out. One that needs no preparation is to review the last few days, weeks or months to gain an overview of your habitual outlook. With a sufficiently unbiased look at behaviour, mental and physical, it is obvious what positive and negative states of mind are most common.

If, on such retrospection, you realise that you suffer a lot from grouchiness, from disaffection, from a general feeling of malaise, and often feel slightly 'flat' or off-colour, then it is probable that there is habitually considerable hatred around. If your life seems grey, if you suffer from depression, those too are good indicators that there is hatred and ill will in your make-up. If you are excessively fussy and neat or if you are prone to criticise others, then that almost certainly points to the root of hatred as a well-established mental characteristic.

Other things indicating the presence of hatred include experiencing a lot of annoyance, anger and resentment. Perhaps you often wake up feeling tense and irritable, with your body uncomfortable, stiff and painful. On the mental front, you may find fault with everything and everyone. If someone speaks to you, you 'bite their head off' without thinking, not even realising at the time that you are being extreme in your reactions.

You may feel a complete aversion from people; you do not want to contact anybody and avoid people whenever you can. Seeing someone you know coming down the street, you cross over to the other side and pretend you have not seen him so you do not have to talk.

You would rather indulge in a sort of bitter solitude, which illustrates the fact that the mark of hatred is aversion, turning away from, not wanting anything to do with.

These attitudes are counteracted by the practice of loving-kindness meditation. If you practise it, if you make much of it, if you cause it to blossom within your character, then you will reduce to a great degree the incidence of ill will and hatred. The practice of loving-kindness is the road to success if ill will is your problem and you seek harmony and happiness in the world.

Success in loving-kindness meditation is marked by a growing absence of annoyance. You become more easy-going, tolerant and are more often than not likely to give others the benefit of the doubt—in great contrast to the earlier habit of constant criticism. You find within yourself a capacity for love and kindness, for consideration, that you never knew was possible.

If freedom of mind is properly developed through loving-kindness, it is impossible that ill will or hatred could invade the mind and persist. The Buddha put it like this. 'Monks, suppose a monk were to say this: "Of a truth, I have developed freedom of mind through loving-kindness, made an increase of it, made a vehicle of it, made a home of it, dwelt with it, gathered it together, set it going—yet ill will invades my mind and stays." Speak to him and say, "Give over, speak not so, reverend sir. Do not distort the word of the Buddha. It is wrong to distort his words thus. Truly, the Exalted One would never speak so. It is not possible, sir, nor could it happen that when freedom of mind is developed through loving-kindness, made an increase of, made a vehicle of, made a home of, dwelt with, gathered together and set well going, that ill will can invade one's mind and stay. It is not possible. Indeed, sir, just this is the escape from ill will—I mean, freedom of mind through loving-kindness." '

This is the first impossibility: anyone who practises loving-kindness and develops it well finds it impossible that ill will could enter the mind and stay there. It may arise—it is certain to, from time to time—but it goes so quickly that it is never a problem.

If you experience many vicious thoughts, the practice of compassion will remove them, for it counters cruelty. How do you know if you experience vicious thoughts? If you have violent and destructive tendencies, if you entertain thoughts of revenge, of harming, of destruction, then you can be certain that there is a streak of cruelty in your nature. If someone upsets you, you might imagine hurting him and be pleased at the thought of his pain and discomfort. If someone stands in your way—maybe of a job promotion or an opportunity—you may picture him dying in an accident or a disaster, thus leaving the way clear for your advancement. Maybe you have a taste for violence—some people find enjoyment by picturing themselves torturing and killing, or raping and pillaging.

These thoughts are far more common than most people would admit. If they are there, then compassion will deal with them. Making much of compassion in the way that I outlined for loving-kindness, living with it, developing it, making a home of it, will eliminate the vicious thoughts so that they can never invade the mind and stay.

Success in the development of the meditation on compassion is marked by the absence of cruelty and violent, vicious thoughts. Even if they do arise, it is for a brief time only; they are easily dismissed and are not a danger in the way that they once were. One becomes kind instead of cruel, helpful instead of obstructive, and acts to reduce the distress of others where possible. Knowing the extremes of cruelty and compassion, it becomes easy to distinguish between them; one would not mistake the compassionate insistence of the stern task-master for cruelty but would see it in its true light: action taken for the ultimate welfare of other beings. It is impossible, if one does develop compassion to its fullest flight, that vicious thoughts can enter the mind and stay. I call this the second impossibility.

Sympathetic joy, delight in the success of others, is the third of the four *Brahma-vihāra*, the divine abidings. If you experience a great deal of envy, the practice of sympathetic joy is the one that is best suited for you, for it overcomes that negative trait. How do you know if envy is a problem for you? If you often experience mental states of contempt or malice or self-pity and are always looking at things with a 'sour-grapes' attitude, then it is certain that you could with profit practise sympathetic joy. Other states occurring that also respond particularly well to the practice of sympathetic joy are dislike, derision and resentment of others' successes.

The development of these mental skills is not easy for, often, our conditioning tends in the opposite direction. We would rather criticise than praise, ridicule rather than help, and envy rather than be pleased at someone else's good fortune. We are constantly beset by our own negative characteristics and have to battle hard to overcome them.

For example, envying and trying to belittle the success of others is common and observable in many very ordinary situations. A friend has bought a new car. You say, 'But didn't you know the "Which?" report said that this car was dangerous?' Envying his success, you devalue his purchase to make yourself feel better. A friend has just got married. You say, 'Did you know statistics say that nowadays one in three marriages ends in divorce?' Unhappy that your friend has found the happiness you seek, you attempt to undermine his happiness. It is not a very pleasant thing to do but, for some, it happens constantly. If, even occasionally, you indulge in these sorts of activities, then you could with profit practise the divine abiding of sympathetic joy, the art of rejoicing in others' good fortune.

Success in that practice brings intense gladness when others do well, when they find fulfilment or happiness or success. Most of the time, there is a complete absence of envy and resentment, and you rarely if ever wish for anything for yourself. For example, if someone you know has a huge win on the National Lottery, you would not think of or expect anything to come your way; you would simply be glad for their success. If their success lies in overcoming personal obstacles or in discovering and practising the Dhamma, then those are great causes for celebration in this way.

If, with a great deal of dedicated effort, one does develop sympathetic joy fully, making a lot of it, coming to success in it, then it is impossible that envy and resentment can invade the mind and stay there. Those unhappy states will arise from time to time, until enlightenment is attained, but they will never stay, for they will be easily replaced by sympathetic joy. That is the third impossibility.

The last of the *Brahma-vihāra* is equanimity. Equanimity counters passion. How do you know if you are a passionate person? If you experience a lot of passionate clinging to craving or hatred, then it is certain that you are a passionate person. If you get extremely troubled and emotional about things, whether personal or global, then you are a passionate person.

Some years ago, when I expressed admiration for a Japanese watch, a colleague flew into a ranting rage about the Japanese people and everything they produced. He turned red in the face, becoming almost apoplectic. The rest of us were astonished. I said, 'But you were not even in the war or scarcely even conscious of it—you're much too young. What's this all about?' He launched into another passionate diatribe against the Japanese, the reasons for which never did become clear, and his angry manner dissuaded us from asking. He shouted wildly that it was our duty to avoid Japanese-made goods of any description. Since he was a computer engineer working every day with components of Japanese manufacture, I have no idea how he came to terms with his job.

The passionate response is not limited to foreign imports, of course. It can apply to anything you can think of—family affairs, crime and punishment, politics and religion are obvious examples. These are the kinds of passions countered by the *Brahma-vihāra* of equanimity. If you practise the divine abiding of equanimity well, if you build it up, make much of it and come to success in it, then you develop neutrality, impartiality towards all beings. This impartiality extends to all things, and includes equanimity towards all the good and all the evil that people visit on the world. You become undismayed by the world, though remaining aware of its problems and successes.

The development of equanimity is not in any way to blind yourself through ignorance to the ills of the world. It is one thing to be indifferent because you do not know what is taking place, and quite another to be completely settled, calm and undismayed though you know the objective facts.

If one develops freedom of mind through equanimity, makes much of it, it is impossible that passion could invade one's mind and stay. I have called this the fourth impossibility.

Each *Brahma-vihāra* confers all eleven benefits listed earlier while at the same time countering a specific mental quality. Their worth is impossible to overestimate. The *Brahma-vihāra* make living in the world a very much more rewarding experience than harbouring passionate craving or malevolence. They cannot remove suffering altogether, however, for they are firmly based in a dualistic view of the world, dealing with beings, with perceptions of good and evil and with extremes.

To purify the mind further, we have to go beyond the perception of separate beings and separate things; we have to go beyond merely cultivating the good. To purify the mind further we have to overcome craving for any dualistic state or thing, the acquisition of which, we believe, would end all our problems. In practice, this means overcoming craving for anything at all and can be accomplished only through gaining insight into reality itself. Insight can be developed only through the practice of *vipassanā* meditation.

Vipassanā is a meditation designed to overcome our conditioned reliance on certain faulty perceptions. Specifically, we tend to perceive things as permanent, satisfactory and self or belonging to self. The practice of *vipassanā* depends on the cultivation of unbiased attentiveness to the fundamental 'building blocks' of experience. We examine our experience directly to see if things are as permanent as we had believed and find that in reality everything is transient. Indeed, it is so fleeting there is nothing we can do with it, which is utterly unsatisfactory. Anything we observe in this way, we find to be dependent on a myriad of other factors; it is not a discrete entity. This applies not only to things in the general sense, but also to those aspects that we believe constitute the 'self'. None of these exist independently of conditions; they are all non-self (*anattā*), just like everything else, and the so-called self is seen to be nothing but a mistaken idea.

Through the meditation, we perceive the true nature of things and this new way of seeing, this new information, brings the realisation that our previous ideas about the world were wrong. In this way, *vipassanā* meditation counters all characteristics of things, or signs, but specifically the signs of permanence, satisfactoriness and self. We no longer believe that things will bring us the happiness we seek.

If we make much of *vipassanā*, if we practise it, develop it fully and attain the necessary insights, we gain the capacity eventually to experience the 'signless' (*animitta*). This is a state of consciousness the predominant feature of which is the absence of the 'signs' of permanence, satisfactoriness and self. Retrospectively contrasting that experience with our normal consciousness—with all the signs in operation—allows us through informed comparison to find out why and how the one is better than the other. We discover the peacefulness of the signless, understand clearly why it is peaceful, realise that it is not a state of annihilation, as many wrongly believe, and thereby strengthen our confidence in the teaching of the Buddha.

If one develops freedom of mind through the signless, it is then impossible that one's mind would run after signs, that it should seek permanence, satisfaction and self in the dualistic world. As the Buddha said, 'For just this is the escape from signs, namely, the signless itself.' This is the fifth impossibility.

There are, however, two kinds of signless. One is created, is brought into being, by the skilful mind of the _vipassanā_ meditator through his or her strenuous efforts to follow the course of practice properly. The other is free from this limitation; it is uncreated, unproduced, unconditioned in any way. It is not a product or result of meditation or of anything else. This is the signless that we have been seeking all along and, knowing this, the skilful meditator eventually leaves behind the 'mind-produced signless' for the genuine article.

When realisation comes, as it must in the end having practised in the right way, there is total freedom from all ideas and feelings of self and, with that, complete freedom from all questions and all doubt. 'It is impossible that someone correctly says, "I am free of the thought 'I am', yet doubts and questionings arise and invade my mind." For just this is the escape from doubt and questioning, namely, the complete rooting out of the thought "I am".' That is the sixth impossibility.

The Buddha's eightfold path is a means of bringing one's life into line with reality. It can be summed up in the verse found in the _Dhammapada_: 'Cease to do evil; cultivate the good; purify the mind. This is the teaching of all Buddhas.' One ceases to do evil through living by the precepts. One cultivates the good by practising loving-kindness, compassion, sympathetic joy and equanimity. One purifies the mind by practising _vipassanā_ and cultivating the signless, eventually to attain complete liberation, _nibbāna_, the deathless, the highest happiness.

7

The Problem of Fear

In London in the early seventies, an elderly meditator was mugged going home from an evening meeting. She was terribly shocked—by the violence more than by the loss of her handbag. She became so distressed that she would not go out at all unless accompanied by a friend.

These days there is a new twist. A young man walking through his local town at lunchtime was startled when a car screeched to a halt by his side. The passenger jumped out, pointed a gun at him, demanded that he hand over his new and very expensive jacket, jumped back in the car and was driven off at speed.

Are things really getting worse, as older people say constantly, or are the problems the same as they always have been?

The world is certainly changing: there are more of us for one thing, and overcrowding definitely brings with it some social problems. The real problem, however, is fear.

Who knows what the next few years may bring? Whose job is secure today? Poverty seems to be increasing right across the country. Crime is certainly on the increase. War and pollution stalk the entire planet. Famine and starvation seem to be constantly in the news. Economies are collapsing. The world looks to be in a decidedly sorry state—but is it any worse than it was?

There have been plenty of bad times in the past—the Great Depression, to mention but one. Even worse, these islands have been invaded many times. Looking it up, I found that we have been invaded *and occupied* at different times by the Gauls, the Romans, the Angles, the Saxons, the Vikings and the Normans. Not only that but, as a nation, we have been involved in so many wars that it is difficult to count them.

Are we to suppose that in all of these things there was no trauma for ordinary folk? It hardly seems likely. Currently we are in a peaceful period—yet it seems to me that people are more afraid than ever.

There are several common fears and anxieties. One condition afflicting many of us today is a sense of futility. It arises based on fear that any effort we might make towards personal fulfilment is ultimately doomed to failure. For many of my generation, the triggering factor was fear of the bomb. It seemed that no matter how hard we worked, no matter what efforts we might put in to establish our careers, families and home-life, it could all be brought to a very untimely end by some zealous hothead pushing a red button.

The things we fear may have changed, but the fear seems to remain a constant. Today, it is fear of pollution, or of the results of global warming, that affects people most. Pollution implies damage to our health and to that of our children; it threatens the environment, including all plant, animal and bird life. It looks as if the world is under a threat it may never have faced before.

Pollution has many causes but is fundamentally due to ever-expanding populations. We are losing the very lungs of the planet as rain forests are cut down to provide room for increasing numbers of people. The ozone layer is being damaged and skin cancer is on the increase. Global warming might bring permanent flooding, reducing the amount of land available for people to live on, increasing population density yet further and making things many times worse. More people, more waste, more pollution. Is it any wonder that many today feel powerless to stop the disasters that seem to be looming over us all?

Today, people fear violence from their fellows in a way that seems to be relatively new in modern, Western society. Women are taught to 'get in touch with their anger' and urged to carry defensive weapons and alarms in their handbags. Householders fit locks and bars. The police carry killing weapons. People carry telephones in their cars to call for assistance without running the risk of leaving the relative safety of the vehicle. One person, on his own, cannot change this state of affairs—and that recognition can be the origin of a sense of futility, a fear of being powerless.

Another fear common today is that of being worthless. In the late eighties, there was relatively little redundancy. Today, in the mid-nineties, if you have not been made redundant yourself, you are certain to know someone—probably someone close to you—who has. Being unable to find work is distressing in the extreme; having nothing to offer that anyone wants inevitably leads an individual to question his value to society. Feeling worthless can lead to all kinds of problems. Among the young, it can provoke vandalism and violence or, if less extraverted, depression or suicide. Low self-esteem—fearing oneself to be inferior to others—seems to be a growing problem.

On another tack, many fear intimacy, believing that in showing tenderness, for example, they display weakness. It takes courage to make ourselves vulnerable to other human beings, to be open; often we fear ridicule or personal disadvantage too much to expose ourselves to such imagined danger.

If we constantly indulge such fears, we can end up afraid of almost everything. It can get to the point that fear has such a grip that we no longer know what we are afraid of. Extreme anxiety seems constantly present and takes a heavy toll on mind and body by way of hyper-tension, hyperalertness and general stress. What can we do?

The Buddha's teaching is designed to eliminate all anguish, including all kinds of fear. It shows how fear arises, the peril in it and the escape from it. While there appear to be many fears—of heights, of enclosed spaces, of open spaces, of water, of spiders, snakes and even pigeons, to mention but a few not touched on so far—the mechanism of fear is the same in every case. The arising of any fear follows exactly the same rules, the experience itself is the same, and the escape from the fear is the same.

For convenience, we can divide fear at the conventional level into two kinds: rational and irrational. Rational fear is based on a real possibility of danger, whereas irrational fear is based on fantasy, on wrong ideas about the object.

Pollution, for example, is a real possibility, a real danger; our children may suffer from it more than we do. The house we live in could burn down. We could be run down crossing the road. In most of these cases, we can do something about the cause of our worry. We can fit smoke alarms and take out house insurance. We can teach our children how properly to cross the road. We can try to minimise any pollution it is under our power to control. These measures will help to settle the mind and banish the fear.

With personal matters, the same approach also works very well. Worried about toothache? Don't put it off; go to the dentist. Your mind will be set at rest, whatever you find. Has your partner become emotionally distant? Ask what is wrong; talk. Whatever you discover, you will at least know. Your mind will be set at rest to that extent.

The trouble is that we tend to ignore our fears and worries because we desperately fear personal discomfort and painful feelings. We would rather put up with the torture of fear than face changes that may be painful. Nowhere is this truer than with relationships, which account for so much suffering in the world. If we were to face the problems squarely, we would find that, in many cases, they would be far less severe than we imagined.

Why does fear arise? While many may agree that certain things are fearful, we are so diverse as human beings that it is by no means true for all of us. We do not all fear the same things; what is terrifying for one is of no consequence for another. Fear, then, cannot be due to the object itself; if it were we would all without exception find the same things frightening.

Fear arises mainly because we see the wrong things as important; we attach our ambitions, our ideas of success or security, to things that are bound to fail us. The most obvious of these are concerned with the material world. For example, we might make our ambition the amassing of material wealth or goods, the attainment of security or to keep the appearance of youth. Never far away is fear of loss, fear of insecurity, fear of ageing or death itself.

Alternatively, we seek comfort and sensual indulgence before all else. In this case, fear arises on painful experiences, illness or privation—things that are scarcely avoidable in some measure no matter where or how we live. Seeing the wrong things as important means that we have a world-view that is significantly inaccurate or incomplete. In fact, all fears arise on fantastic or incorrect views of the world.

The most important of the wrong views upon which fear arises is that the body is the self. Most hold the belief: 'I am the physical body, the physical body is my self.' For these people, bodily beauty, bodily health and bodily survival are the only criteria of what is truly worthwhile. They think, 'If the body is well, I am well.'

Physical dangers that threaten survival, health or comfort are readily apparent. We all take steps to protect physical well-being through seeking adequate food, shelter and clothing. For continued peace of mind, we seek assurance that those things will continue—hence insurance, pensions and investments.

The logical extension of the belief that the body is the self is that this life is the only one we have. It implies that there is nothing apart from bodily existence and that death is complete annihilation of body and mind. It follows that those who believe the body is the self will cling to physical existence with maniacal strength. Any threat to physical well-being suggests to them the possibility of complete annihilation. Fear grows in direct proportion to the craving for more material security and safety.

If the body were the self, then the death of the body would be the end of the self, of 'me', the end of everything, annihilation. If the body-self were to be the only one we have, death would mark the end of all life. Death would truly be the great destroyer of dreams. It would be bottomless oblivion with no way back—a truly fearful prospect.

In parallel with the belief that the body is the self, many people in the West believe only in physical causes and results. Effectively limiting action to the body, the only criterion of success is what you can get away with; there can be no disadvantage to theft, for instance, unless you are caught. It is not significant that your mind is a hell of fear and anxiety, as long as you can put up a front that fools other people. There is no room in such a world-view for mental actions and results.

I once studied with an astrology teacher who fancied herself as something of a philosopher. She asked her students to imagine an action that ultimately would be harmless to anyone. When everyone had replied—and some of the answers were extremely strange—she gave her considered idea of a harmless action. It was to sit alone in a room and write a vitriolic hate letter to someone you knew—and then to tear it up and throw it away. Why, in her view, was it harmless? Because no one would know—you would not be found out. For her, it was only physical things, tangible things, which were important. She was ignorant of the peril of harbouring hatred in the mind and of the dire results of mental action based on it.

To gain security from at least the more obvious forms of fear and suffering, it is necessary to correct any wrong views or opinions you hold. Of necessity, this means to adopt mundane right view.

The Buddha taught five points of view that make up the most accurate world-view it is possible to have.

The first of these is 'There is action and result.' This statement refers to the law of *kamma*: physical, verbal or mental actions have results directly relating to their ethical component. Briefly, performing selfish actions—those accompanied by craving or hatred—brings you suffering; unselfish actions bring nothing but pleasant states.

The second point is an extension of the first: 'There is a result of giving.' The act of generosity is of immense benefit—to the giver. While the recipient clearly benefits, the main point here is that the ethical action of generosity is of great value to the person performing it, producing real benefits of many different kinds, including wealth and popularity.

The third right view is 'There are mother and father.' This terse statement draws attention to the fact that parents are worthy of the greatest consideration and respect for bringing us into the world in the first place and for providing us with all we need to become fully-functioning human beings.

The fourth point of mundane right view is 'There are spontaneously arisen beings.' Other realms and the beings that populate them do exist; they are not figments of the imagination or other levels of consciousness within our minds. Other realms do exist; they are real places where we ourselves may arise after death, subsequently to live and die. Equally, beings on those other levels may be reborn here, in the human realm; other realms are not eternal heavens, merely other habitats where beings live for a shorter or longer time.

And the fifth point: 'There are men and women who know about these things from their own experience and can teach us about them.'

Some say these ideas are not scientific because there is no objective proof of their validity. There is, however, a great deal of supporting evidence, much of it common-sense or commonplace. Who lives more happily, the murderer or the man who stays his hand? Who experiences the greater dread, the thief or the honest man? Who is the more afraid, the individual who thinks death is complete annihilation or someone convinced there is another life? For those who practise meditation and study the Buddha's teachings, there is plenty of incontrovertible evidence of the reality of 'action and result' in the form of personal experience. As far as the reality of 'spontaneously arisen beings' is concerned, there exist meditation practices through which a sufficiently dedicated and skilled meditator can find out for himself.

Ask any meditator who has been keeping the precepts and practising for some while whether life is better now than it was. The reply will always be a definite affirmative. Restraining inefficient action through keeping the precepts, instituting positive action through meditation, particularly loving-kindness (*mettā*), will always result in an improvement to one's lot in life. This is not a matter of opinion for it is provable by anyone who cares to make the effort. There is much more to life than mere bodily existence.

Of course, many do look deeper than the physical. They discover a yearning that can only be described as spiritual. When this occurs, finding proof that certain kinds of actions bring certain kinds of results becomes of little consequence. Now that the mind is dominated by the need to satisfy the longing for the highest, the search for a way to freedom begins in earnest.

Of the systems that lead to freedom, Buddha-Dhamma, the teaching of the Buddha, is in my view the finest but, in common with others, it needs unswerving commitment if the seeker is to succeed.

To commit ourselves to the Buddha's path, we have to go for refuge to the Buddha, the Dhamma (all of it: not just the bits that agree with our Western conditioning) and the Sangha. These are a real refuge, a sanctuary, a place of safety amid difficult conditions, for they either point the way to freedom from fear and suffering or help us sustain our efforts on the way to that freedom.

To take refuge in the Buddha is to accept that he was a human being who exhibited qualities to which we can all aspire. Further, he discovered a path to freedom and, through compassion for 'those with little dust in their eyes', spent the rest of his life teaching others. Recollection of the historical man can give us great strength of enthusiasm and faith to pursue the path. The word *buddha* literally means enlightenment and, at a more subtle level, taking refuge in *buddha* is to dedicate oneself to realising enlightenment, freedom from all suffering whatever.

The Dhamma is the Buddha's teaching, both conventional and ultimate, that shows a way to the beyond. To take refuge in the Dhamma is to forsake all other teachings and seek sanctuary only within what the Buddha taught. This is in no way to be construed as being narrow-minded; abandoning eclecticism is necessary if one's energies are to be fully engaged in an effective search for freedom from fear and anxiety. It is a fact that attempting to compare one 'religious' way with another leads only to confusion.

Sangha is literally translated as 'community' and has various shades of meaning. The first is the *ariya* Sangha, 'the eight kinds of men and women'—those fully enlightened or certain to become so, those who have direct experience, even if only a glimpse, of the beyond. In a wider sense, the Sangha includes all those under full-time training, whether they have any meditative attainments of that sort or not. Wider still, the Sangha includes all who follow the eightfold path, ordained or lay, full-time or part-time. To take refuge in the Sangha can mean any of these but the first choice is to take refuge in those who know for themselves the freedom from fear and anxiety, freedom from suffering. Those who know the goal by direct experience are in a far better position to guide others when compared with those who have only heard or read of it.

Having taken refuge in the Buddha, Dhamma and Sangha, for best results a seeker needs to follow the eightfold path with commitment and dedication. Pursued faithfully, this wonderful teaching fully justifies its ancient name, the way to heaven. Ultimately, it will free the practitioner from all fear and all suffering.

The foundation of the path is restraint of actions of body, speech and mind. If the meditator is determined, it is not so difficult to ensure that physical behaviour is impeccable. If we do make the effort, we find that restraint calms the mind. Impeccable ethical action removes the basis for guilt and for certain types of fear, notably the fear of being found out.

But calmness of mind cannot be won if our speech is destructive. Destructive speech is any kind of talking, writing or indication intended to threaten friendships, harm reputations and cause hurt or damage to another. It includes lying, slander, gossip and tale-bearing, as well as harsh and angry speech that is offensive.

We have also to restrain actions of mind. Meditation depends greatly upon restraint of the senses, which in turn depends greatly on mental restraint. Restraining the mind is perhaps the most effective and powerful weapon we have in our fight against fear.

As mindfulness improves, it becomes possible actually to see the way in which the senses operate. We see something—maybe an article of clothing in a shop window. In the blink of an eye, we convince ourselves that it is something we absolutely must have. Even if we try to resist, saying, 'This longing is stupid—I know I don't really need it', the image haunts us to such an extent that we cannot resist going into the shop 'just to try it on'. Having gone this far, it is no surprise that we often end up buying something we do not need—and probably feeling guilty about it.

The process is similar for all desirable objects. Having seen something and found it desirable, the urge to act on that desire is almost irresistible. But it is only *almost* irresistible; we do not have to do it. We can restrain ourselves and, most of the time, we all know we can. Some would initially claim that they cannot help themselves but, as mindfulness grows, they realise that is no longer a tenable excuse. Any competent meditator *knows* that cravings can be resisted with mindfulness and determination.

Craving and fear are closely linked. Desperately wanting something, there is fear of not getting it. Craving to maintain an enjoyable state of affairs, there is fear of losing it. Craving to maintain bodily existence at all costs, fear of danger or death can become extreme.

Before he discovered the way to freedom, Siddhattha Gotama, the man who later became Buddha, was concerned about the fear that would occasionally arise in his mind. Determined to conquer it, he used to go into the forest at night, to the loneliest and most frightening places he could find. There he would practise control of his mind, pacing up and down or sitting with his back to a tree. Every time a twig cracked or a leaf rustled, he could see fear trying to grip his mind. If he gave in to it, he knew he would run in panic.

He was determined to master his reactions. Whenever fear arose, he drove it out by mental effort. If he was walking up and down, he continued to walk up and down and fight the fear until he had banished it from his mind and was calm again. If he was sitting down when fear arose, he stayed there and fought it. Determined not to give in he discovered, as will anyone who tries hard enough, that fear is only almost irresistible.

In north-eastern Thailand today there are still tigers in the forests. I have heard that, sometimes, local monks are told to sit on a known tiger-path to meditate. Fear is a likely companion, but they are instructed not to move if a tiger should come along. Fear is only almost irresistible—and cannot exist when loving-kindness fills the mind.

Actions of mind are very important and nowhere more so than in meditation. If your practice is mired in the swamps of boredom or superficiality, for example, try setting up your resolve, try mastering the mind with the mind. Recapture your determination to find the answers. Spend a little time recollecting how keen you used to be, remembering why you meditate. You will find that it is possible to revitalise even the most flagging meditation practice. You do not have to give in to fear, boredom, anxiety or fantasy; you can master all of them.

Mental restraint comes into its own in the attempt to master the passionate response. This is an extreme emotional reaction to apparent success or failure in the meditation. Most meditators instantly recognise the description, for this obstacle arises for everyone near the beginning of any meditative path.

Elation and depression occur in two modes. The most common, at first, is the negative passionate response. The meditation seems to be going well but then you awake with a start and realise that you have dozed off again, in spite of all your efforts. With that recognition, you fall into a pit of despair and self-pity, wondering how you are ever going to get it right. It is all going wrong, it is never going to go right, you might just as well give up, you might just as well jump off a cliff right now. It can take a considerable time to recover your mental balance and re-establish effective meditation.

The other mode of the passionate response is to become elated and excited about momentary success in the meditation—perhaps concentration arises, or calm, or clarity of observation. Whatever it is, the response is one of extreme anticipation and self-congratulation and the mind becomes so disturbed that mental balance is impossible to achieve. Meditators can take a long time to settle down after reacting in this way to what they believed was a 'breakthrough'.

As mindfulness and clear comprehension grow, it is possible to see exactly how the passionate response arises. In the first case, the negative response, it works like this. There is recognition of sleepiness followed immediately by comparison with an image of what you regard as perfect meditation. Grasping at the failure, you identify with it saying, 'This is what I really am; I am useless, a failure. I will never be able to meditate successfully.'

Exactly the same principle applies with elation. If you judge the meditation to have gone well, excitement and elation arise like fireworks in the mind. Again, this is due to comparison and subsequent grasping at the image of the successful state. You identify with it and say to yourself, 'This is what I want. I can do it. I am getting to be a superb meditator.' The mind becomes so agitated that the stability of the meditation is shattered. The disturbance can be so great that you do not settle down for days, doing no useful work in the interim.

With further training, these problems can be avoided. You do not have to grasp at the success or failure. If you simply acknowledge—note—what is happening and refuse to be drawn in, you can avoid problems altogether. Whether the passionate response is one of despair or elation, it can be addressed in the same way as fear. The passionate response, like fear, is only almost irresistible. You can restrain the mind from elation; you can restrain the mind from depression. Elation and depression always signify self-indulgence and, when that is present, no useful meditation is done.

Most dedicated meditators master the passionate response, though the time taken varies greatly from person to person. Once clear of its disruptive influence, truly meditative insight arises in the unhindered mind. Things are seen increasingly clearly as transient. The entire world is perceived—directly experienced—as fragile, as incapable of supporting anything lasting. This is not an idea, it is not an intellectual understanding; it is direct and unmistakable experience. Trying to describe such insights, a meditator may say that it feels as if he is standing on a sheet of very thin ice and that, no matter in which direction he looks, there is no solid land in sight.

To experience the entire world dissolving moment to moment generates great fear; everything in the mental and physical environment is experienced as fearful. Again, this is not an idea. It is not an intellectual assessment that things are fearful but a direct and

unmistakable experience that is undeniable. Sometimes, meditators
neglect to restrain their minds at this point and are severely troubled
about their meditation. The fear seems nearly overwhelming and
inescapable—but it is only nearly overwhelming. When reminded
about restraint and the peril in self-indulgence, the fear is seen for
what it is—a true response of the conditioned mind to the recognition that nothing lasts for more than an instant.

Under normal circumstances, we suppress the understanding of
transience by ignoring it as hard as we can. We do not want to know
that the things we wrongly think so important and for which we
work so hard are actually as ephemeral as mist on a summer morning.
We think that if we were to admit this to ourselves, life would not be
worth living. In that, we are wrong. Wherever there is ignore-ance
there is craving; where there is craving, there is always fear. Craving
to possess is always aligned with fear of loss; it cannot be otherwise.
Craving for sensual pleasure is always allied with fear of unpleasant or
painful feelings—always. Craving for progress is always bound up
with fear of failure—always; it cannot be otherwise.

With faith in the Buddha, the Dhamma and the Sangha, fear is
only a temporary obstacle. We who walk the eightfold path restrain
our anti-social activities and develop positive actions, such as
generosity and loving-kindness, laying a firm foundation for the
attempt to conquer fear of all kinds. Through training the mind in
the art of meditation, we learn how to restrain mental indulgence,
including the restraint of depression, elation and fear itself.

The meditator who understands fear understands craving and, with
that understanding, turns away from both. Seeing transience clearly it
becomes impossible to crave for anything and, where there is no
craving, there can be no fear. Where there is no craving and no fear
there is no problem internally; the mind is at rest and peace reigns in
place of fear and anxiety.

But how do you cope when your house burns down or the cat is
sick on your best shirt? What happens when you lose a loved one
before his or her time, through illness, violence or accident? These
things are real problems in the conventional sense and, as far as the
external world is concerned, overcoming fear has changed nothing.
Problems still occur; they cannot be avoided.

The trained meditator sees far more deeply than convention allows.

Even before the end of the training, meditators begin to realise that the conventional world is just as transient, just as momentary, as things experienced in meditation. The conventional world is an uncertain, fearful place. People do die, cats are inconveniently sick, houses do burn down. This is the way of things. All the precautions in the world can never shelter us completely from things we do not like. The trained meditator fully accepts everything that happens. He knows that all this must pass and refuses to allow fear or anxiety to grip his mind.

Fear is a problem only for the untrained mind. For those who have taken the trouble to learn about themselves, to practise restraint and to overcome the passionate response, fear can never again be the problem it once was. Ultimately, with the successful conclusion of the meditative path, fear is eliminated forever, along with every vestige of suffering.

8

Beginnings and Endings

Beginnings and endings are very important to us.

The birth of a baby is a happy event. Marriage is often solemnised in church or temple and celebrated by a lavish feast, with music and dancing to help the food and drink go down. We mark with ceremony and ostentation the opening of a show, an inauguration, the beginning of a new venture—indeed, the beginning of anything that we regard as significant. Each New Year is seen in with much revelry. A beginning seems to symbolise fresh hope, a new start when all will be well.

Endings are equally important. People go to great lengths to attend the funeral of a relative they have not seen for years. Retirement from working life is often celebrated. Farewells—typically on leaving one job or country for another—are occasions for celebration and revelry mixed with tears. The end of the year, the coming of the shortest day at the winter solstice, is widely celebrated. Now called Christmas, once called Saturnalia, it is a time to make merry, to drink to the death of the old year and toast the prospect of lengthening days.

We all feel the importance of beginnings and endings.

Even those of us who see life as a series of cycles still distinguish beginnings and endings. Farm workers are more conscious of the seasons than the years—or were so, before farming became industrial business and financial years came to such prominence. Some, particularly in agrarian communities in parts of Asia, mark time by lunar months, by the cycles of the moon. We can see remnants of this in the ceremonies of traditional Buddhism where *uposattha* days, days of *puja* and increased meditative activity, are marked by the quarters of the moon. In countries like our own, the working week is a familiar cycle—with the end of the week often celebrated, if not the beginning.

We are all familiar with the daily round. Newspapers are published every twenty-four hours, and events reported on that cycle. News that is more than twenty-four hours old is old news indeed.

Longer cycles abound. Sunspots have one cycle of eleven years and another of twenty-two. The Chinese astrological calendar is based on a twelve-year cycle. According to both science and cosmology there are infinitely long cycles during which the entire universe evolves and devolves, aeon after aeon. There is periodic renewal, periodic destruction, on and on, through measureless time.

Some are drawn to look for an ultimate beginning; they want to find out where everything began, the 'first cause'. Was there, at the very beginning, something or someone that started the universe in motion? Was there a 'big bang', a cataclysmic cosmic event, an inconceivable explosion of dense matter that, in expanding and cooling, has produced the universe as we know it today? Even here, some prefer to think in terms of cycles. The big bang and subsequent expansion are only the latest of many; there have been countless expansions and contractions stretching back into the infinite past.

When we look at life within the universe, we are faced with a similar conundrum. Does each life begin at birth, starting from nothing more than the conjoined genetic material of mother and father? Is that the 'first cause' of human existence—or can we look at this too in terms of cycles? Most of the world believes in rebirth or reincarnation—wandering from life to life in an endless round of birth and death. It is this we call *samsāra*.

This process of rebirth is not random but conditioned by the actions we have performed in the past. Choosing to act selfishly, we generally end up worse off next time round; acting wisely, we find ourselves in happier circumstances. In effect, we choose the general tenor of our next lifetime. Indeed, some authorities maintain that we choose not only the circumstances of our rebirth in terms of it being better or worse, but also the time period in which to be reborn. Instead of being reborn in the near future, one could choose the fourteenth century, perhaps, or the twenty-ninth.

To seek an ultimate beginning of life is to flirt with madness. Such a search can lead only to an infinite regress, with every furthest point being found to depend on something before it—back and ever backwards with no conceivable end. We can never know what was the ultimate beginning of things, where it all began, for whatever we find has to be supported by something else behind it. Anything we find has to have come from something else, for nothing can exist of itself.

Philosophers, well aware of the problem of infinite regress, know that it is not possible to penetrate behind first assumptions, that it is possible to demonstrate logically only that which was assumed in the first place. Logic cannot go beyond itself. A first beginning is forever beyond reach. To test our assumptions, we have to go beyond logic into the realm of direct experience.

The Buddha was fully aware of these issues. He was concerned only with the arising and ending of suffering (*dukkha*). He made no claim to show where life and the world began and explicitly avoided the topic as one of the great unanswerable questions. Instead, he focused on the origin and cessation of suffering due to conditions, dealing with what could be proven here and now—through direct experience—to be the case. He never claimed to show where life and the world would end and expressly classified the topic as irrelevant, as another of the great unanswerable questions. His sole concern was to teach the arising and ending of suffering due to conditions.

He said, 'If this is, that comes to be; from the arising of this, that arises. If this is not, that does not come to be; from the stopping of this, that is stopped.' He expanded this enigmatic statement in the famous formula of condition dependent origination (*paticca-samuppāda*) which contains twelve links or conditions arranged in an endless circle, each one conditioning the next. I will not go into detail this evening, but here is an outline so you can see how it works.

In the life before this, ignorance was the major condition for the arising of craving. Actions based on that craving gave rise, after death in that lifetime, to the birth of the mind and body in this lifetime. In this life, our reactions to unavoidable resultants from past actions and to new events are based in ignorance and craving, which are the major conditions for birth into the next life. Once born into that future life, there follows subsequent decay, woe, lamentation, despair and death.

So arises all suffering whatsoever, said the Buddha. This is *samsāra*, the round of birth and death.

In all of this, there is no permanent self. There is no being or self that goes on unchanged from life to life. There are only changing conditions, unfolding and interacting.

In reply to the question 'Who or what is reborn?' the Buddha replied that it was neither the same nor different. If that seems too cryptic, consider waking up in the morning. Are you the same person who went to sleep the night before? Well, yes, in a way—but there again, no: you have changed overnight, being a few hours older for one thing. There is certainly nothing static in the process.

The Buddha pointed out that all suffering in this world arises from the fact of having been born. You cannot experience the distress of a broken relationship, an illness or a redundancy unless you have first been born. It seems obvious, but the definition of birth bears looking at. Birth is not only the adoption of a material body; it is also the psychological adoption of a self in the moment—the arising of the idea of 'me, myself, I' as a separate individual.

Condition dependent origination has far-reaching consequences. To repeat what the Buddha said: 'If this is, that comes to be; from the arising of this, that arises. If this is not, that does not come to be; from the stopping of this, that is stopped.' Putting some flesh on the bones of his statement, he said that if ignorance exists, craving must arise. If craving exists, birth must arise. If birth exists, suffering must arise. If ignorance ceases, craving must cease. If craving ceases, birth cannot arise. If there is no birth there can be no suffering and no death. He said, 'Thus ceases this whole mass of suffering.'

The Buddha's superlative teaching is most definitely not theoretical. It is in essence a series of practical instructions on how to bring about the total cessation of suffering. The Buddha taught a practical and effective way to freedom from all ills.

The way to the complete cessation of suffering is called the noble eightfold path. The eight components of the path fall naturally into three divisions: discipline (*sīla*), meditation (*samādhi*) and wisdom (*paññā*).

The first section that we meet is *sīla* or discipline, which is a matter of attempting to remove or restrain elements of our behaviour harmful to or inconsiderate of others. The usual template lay people work to is that of the five training precepts, while monks and nuns have many more rules to contend with.

Restraining behaviour in these ways calms the mind so that it can begin to work successfully at the second section of the noble eightfold path: *samādhi*, the setting up of mindfulness and concentration. As mindfulness and concentration increase, it becomes possible to observe body and mind in detail, clearly and without bias.

The increasingly subtle observation of all aspects of mind and body provides the ideal foundation for the meditator to develop the third section of the path: *paññā* or wisdom. Wisdom is a matter of developing comprehension through direct experience. Its purpose, in line with the Buddha's single aim of eradicating suffering, is to overcome ignorance. When ignorance is overcome, craving cannot arise, birth cannot arise, death cannot arise and suffering cannot arise. Just this is the end of suffering.

We remain tied to the wheel of endless birth and death for as long as we believe that things are inherently lasting, satisfactory and separate. We actually (mis)perceive mental and material things in this way and these three misperceptions are called the hallucinations of perception (*vipallāsa*) to underline that fact. Progress towards the eradication of all suffering is made through direct observation of the real state of affairs and it is this observation that overcomes the hallucinations.

We observe—directly, through experience—that all conditioned things are transient, unsatisfactory and non-self—the three marks of all conditioned phenomena. It is not enough to acknowledge intellectually the probable truth of statements about the three marks; it is necessary to see, through direct experience, that they are true. While intellectual understanding is important, it is not enough on its own, for it can never re-order perceptions at this most fundamental level. There has to be direct experience of the three marks for progress to be made.

It is only this direct comprehension, this insight, that overcomes ignorance. Overcoming ignorance, it breaks the fetters that bind us to the round of birth and death, to *samsāra*, to suffering itself.

The first three fetters, out of ten in all, are belief in a self, clinging to rule and ritual, and sceptical doubt. They can exist only if ignorance exists. Their elimination is a most important milestone on the journey to freedom. Overcoming the first three fetters marks the point at which a meditator becomes certain of final enlightenment, within a maximum of seven more lifetimes (though, with more work, he or she might be able to succeed in this very lifetime). He becomes a streamwinner; he wins to the stream that flows inexorably to enlightenment.

With more practice, a streamwinner develops the wisdom that destroys ignorance. In doing so, he observes the end of beginnings; there is no more arising of self in the moment. He sees the end of becoming and realises that, as there is now no psychological adoption of self, so there can be no more birth. There is nothing to become, nothing to be born, there are no beginnings. This is true freedom. He is free from the past, free from the future, free from the present and free from views.

He also sees the end of endings—he comes to the deathless. Seeing that all things are *anattā*, non-self, he realises that there is no self to die. In fact, all conditioned things are so transient that it is arguable that they do not exist at all. There is nothing to die; it is the end of endings.

* * *

We have journeyed through an entire universe, seen it in its evil aspect, striven for the good, forsaken that and striven for the spiritual, finally to return to our starting point. It is very different, however. Just as the foreign traveller returns home and sees his old haunts with new eyes, so does the spiritual traveller come home to see it in a totally different way. While appearing the same from the outside, he is altogether different, though this is difficult to convey to others. How do you represent the beauty of a rose to a blind man? Or the song of a nightingale to one born deaf?

The successful spiritual traveller completely understands suffering. He knows through experience its conditioned nature, its origins and its cessation. Having won to the deathless, he knows with a knowing that goes beyond words that he is free, that the universe is love, that his journey is ended and that there is no more to do. He is finally at peace.

9

All You Ever Wanted to Know about the Rise and Fall

The reasons people turn to meditation are extremely varied, but all have one thing in common: a need for solace. Some wish to alleviate the distress arising from a broken relationship or a bereavement. Others long to overcome the frustration they feel from not knowing the deeper meaning of life, death and suffering.

The reason for turning to meditation is one thing, but knowing how to do it is quite another. We are taught that insight meditation is performed by watching the rise and fall of things, but it helps greatly to be clearly aware of what that means. The term 'rise and fall' is used in different contexts and we need to look at some of them to grasp the full extent of this simple but powerful practice.

All external phenomena rise and fall. Mountains, seemingly so permanent, rise as continents collide, and fall as weathering inexorably wears them away over geological ages. Rivers, trees, plants, planets and suns rise and fall. The star we call our sun will eventually explode. Everything has a beginning. Everything has an end. Nothing is excepted, however large, however small. From solar system to virus, all things rise and fall, all things are born and die.

Internally, on a personal level, everything within mind and body has a beginning and an end; it rises and falls. Nothing lasts. We are born, come to growth, decay and die. The human lifespan rarely if ever exceeds a hundred and ten years and, during that time, states of health fluctuate, rising and falling unpredictably. While the body may last for a few decades, the mind changes with almost inconceivable rapidity. Happy one minute, sad the next, we can find nothing lasting in the universe of mind. Always there is rise and fall.

Any of these is a suitable object of contemplation, but there are more and less effective levels of practice.

For meditation to succeed, we need to attend to rise and fall internally and externally. We can attend to transience externally by thinking about long-term decay of mountains or planets, though this is really an intellectual exercise because such changes are not immediately visible. More obvious is the rise and fall of the seasons and the weather.

Also externally, we can observe other people and man-made objects. We see people coming and going along a road, a street, in a room, or we might witness actual birth and death. We can consider the various characteristics of other human beings, analysing their appearance into sensory data that impinge upon us. Whichever way we approach the observation, one thing is clear: anything we pay attention to comes into existence and passes away again, both long-term and, more immediately, as data impinging on the sense-bases.

With material objects that we own, it is no different. Possessions that we say we have had for years are, upon examination, composed of parts that are always decaying through wear and tear, sometimes to be replaced entirely. Trigger, the road-sweeper in *Only Fools and Horses*, was given a municipal award for keeping the same broom for twenty years. When congratulated by his friends, he pointed out that the broom had had 15 new heads and 4 new handles in that time ... In any event, the sight or sound of even the most 'long-lasting' object arises and passes frequently. All things rise and fall.

The way to attend to rise and fall externally is to note that all of these things are transient, that they all rise and pass away. It is not enough to maintain a background understanding that the world is as it is—we need to experience the transience and note for ourselves that none of these things is lasting.

On a personal level, also, it is important to note that things come and go. We need to attend to our own mental and physical states—to attend to transience internally—and remark upon the fact that these things also arise and pass away. Such noting is the very basis of attending to rise and fall in the meditation practice.

Meditation allows us to sharpen our appreciation of transience by focusing intently on the subtle operation of mind and body. The basic practice is to attend to the sensation of the rise and fall of the abdominal area that is brought about dependent upon the breathing process. Although it sounds simple enough, meditators interpret the instruction in a surprising number of ways.

Some people when attending to the rise and fall of the abdomen find a distinct, small and definite sensation that seems to run horizontally in and out, about two-fingers' breadth above the navel. It is as thick as a piece of cotton or string, as it were, and it runs from a point about halfway through the body (back to front) and horizontally out towards the skin surface. They follow this sensation as it goes up—as it rises towards the surface of the body—and falls, going back in towards the centre. They follow it carefully, and become calm and concentrated thereby.

Others, in contrast, find that they are aware of the whole ribcage going in and out and perceive the feeling to be about thirty centimetres in diameter, expanding and contracting with the breathing. Should they attempt a finer focus, they lose the sensation altogether.

Some, rather than experience the feeling of rise and fall internally, locate it on the surface of the skin as it touches their clothing and observe that particular pressure getting stronger and weaker, rising and falling.

Some can feel the surface of the diaphragm as it descends on the in-breath and ascends on the out-breath, feeling a vertical movement about a third of the way into the body from the front and moving up and down through about five or six centimetres.

And then there are those who find the whole thing something of a mystery. They cannot distinguish any abdominal feeling because they are caught up with *thinking* about rise and fall, assuming that is what is meant by attending to rise and fall.

These are some different ways of attending to rise and fall. There are others, but these are the most common.

What is the best way? We have to take into account that each individual is unique. Our past conditioning is so varied that there is no conceivable way we could perceive things identically with one another. Everyone perceives rise and fall—or anything else—differently. Whatever our mode of perception, however, there is one quality we all must have if the meditation is to be effective.

For the most effective meditation, it is necessary to focus with precision on the sensation of rise and fall so that one can clearly follow it increasing and decreasing or rising and falling. Generally, this means sharpening mindfulness and concentration to the point where one can distinguish that sensation while remaining calm and collected. Increasing concentration constrains the thinking process and allows freedom from discursiveness which, in turn, aids the concentration and the ability to focus on the physical feeling.

Whether our primary aim is to gain calm or to develop insight, we need to practise the same basic exercises to start with.

The first step is to define the hindrances to meditation. We have to know what obstacles we are facing, and of what they consist. Eventually, we must learn how to deal with them.

There are five major hindrances. Hindrances are things we do; they are actions we perform to ease a current difficulty. Being habitual, in most cases they are mental actions that we do unknowingly and it is at first difficult to see what we are doing. The actions have become so familiar that they have sunk below the level of consciousness, as it were; and we do them without thinking, without awareness.

Hindrances obscure purity of mind. Purity of mind is not something we develop; it is something that is uncovered once we get rid of the hindrances. We do not have to create it; it is always there behind the superficial mental 'noise' that we are so attached to.

Buddha-Dhamma, the teaching of the Buddha, is without equal in its codified form of instruction. There are four noble truths, five hindrances, six sense-bases, seven factors of enlightenment, eight worldly conditions, nine spheres of being, ten fetters, and many more lists besides. It is well worthwhile learning some of these off by heart for then, during a meditation plagued by hindrances or confusion, a list may come to mind and immediately clarify the problem.

To overcome the hindrances we develop the four right efforts. These are the effort to eradicate negative states already present, the effort to prevent negative states arising, the effort to encourage positive states, and the effort to maintain positive states already in existence. Let me give you some examples.

Sensual desire, indulgence in sensuality, is the first of the five major hindrances.

In a television interview, a man describing his experiences on a meditation retreat wryly remarked that, for him, the retreat had been extremely difficult between meals. This kind of experience is familiar to many and illustrates the prevalence of sensual desire. Trying to gain peace and calm, the mind is perversely filled with thoughts of food: the next meal of the day, meals you have had, meals you are going to prepare when the retreat ends, meals you might eat when on holiday. This goes on for hour after hour of meditation as though there were real and present danger of starvation. Very little if any meditative work is done; the sensual desire seems an insurmountable obstacle to purity of mind, to the calmness and tranquillity, the spaciousness, that could be there in the absence of the hindrances.

Of course, sensual desire applies not only to food but also to every sensual indulgence. One of the most troublesome for many is sex and, as with food, this can seem to be an insuperable obstacle to the meditation. There are, however, standard countermeasures that can be employed. The first is to recognise consciously that you are responsible for the thoughts and that you are choosing to think of these things. The thoughts are not being forced upon you; you are choosing to put energy into them, into the fantasies, the memories and the imaginings. You can withdraw that energy. You can restrain it. While the initial thought of food or sex may arise unbidden, you can refuse to continue thinking of it. This corresponds to the right effort to remove negative or inefficient states of mind already in existence and to the effort to maintain their absence.

Restraint is not enough on its own for, without augmentation from the other right efforts, thinking about food or sex will invariably arise again and the meditation is likely to become either a battleground or full of fantasy. Developing positive or efficient states of mind helps greatly to overcome these problems and one of the best approaches is to concentrate on what you are doing in the moment, to bend the mind in a direction that is positive in respect of the meditation. If you are sitting down, that could be to concentrate on the rise and fall of the abdomen. If you are walking about in between meditations, then concentrate on your walking; pay mindful attention to the actual sensations in the soles of the feet as you walk along. You will find that the mind becomes filled with these things rather than what was troubling you before. It is hard work, and it needs persistence, but the results are fully worth the effort.

The second of the five major hindrances is ill will or hatred. This manifests in different shades, from feeling generally fed up, through mild irritability, all the way to raging anger or cold, implacable hatred. On retreat, you may occasionally become annoyed with the Centre, with yourself and with your fellow meditators. Everywhere you look, you see something to criticise, something wrong, something not as you think it should be. Curiously, people are often unwilling to admit to such states of mind, but they are very common and constitute a most definite obstacle to right meditation.

You can overcome ill will temporarily by a variety of tactics. For instance, ill will can be made to vanish by 'counting your blessings'. It is extraordinarily effective. Consider how well-off you are. You have food in your stomach, a roof over your head, clothes on your back and a comfortable lifestyle judged by the standards of some other places in the world. You are doing what you have always wanted to do, coming to know more about yourself, coming to greater understanding and peace of mind. In recounting these facts, you will find that the mind lightens. The ill will diminishes and disappears. Joy arises, and gladness of mind. If you then do some loving-kindness meditation—to yourself, to the Centre and to the people around you—you can eliminate ill will for the time being. As a strategy, longer-term, loving-kindness meditation also works very well. It predisposes the mind to a friendlier and happier outlook that is reflected in everyday activity. It definitely minimises the occurrence of ill will when practised properly.

Sloth and torpor is a hindrance that troubles most meditators from time to time. It can arise from a number of different conditions and, to deal with it effectively, we have to know its origins. Sloth tends to be comfortable, full of fantasies or daydreams, and can be sleepily pleasant, though never productive. It arises either from simple laziness, lack of application, or from excessive concentration and inadequate mindfulness. In contrast, torpor is stiffness and unworkability of mind arising from too much effort. It is often accompanied by bodily discomfort, such as pressure in the head and pains in the neck and back. It is very common to find the two combined—sleepiness and tension—hence the name for the hindrance.

The way to overcome simple sloth is by trying harder, by putting in more effort and by brightening the mind. The way to overcome torpor, stiffness, is by relaxing, by taking it easy, by developing calmness and tranquillity and of course, most important of all, mindfulness. In both cases, flexibility of mind seems to be an essential factor. The mind with sloth and torpor is reluctant to attend to what is present, becoming locked in on one or another troublesome object.

Increase the mindfulness, note what is happening in mind and body, and the problems tend to fade. In both cases, there is laziness in refusing to modify one's habitual methods of tackling problems.

The fourth major hindrance is agitation or 'flurry and worry'. The mind jumps about from this to that, with so many things going on that you do not know where to turn next. It often arises as planning, and may include concerns about major lifestyle changes, home-decorating or, on a residential course, a forthcoming interview or what to do when you leave. In severe cases, agitation can become so strong that individuals feel sick and may even vomit. As with other hindrances, the key to overcoming it lies in knowing its origins. Agitation is due, always, to excessive effort coupled with lack of mindfulness. In contrast with torpor, it is active, very active, and the problem is not slowness of mind but rather its speed.

Occasionally, a meditator will wrongly identify the hindering agitation as zest or helpful energy. These are the ones who, so keen to progress, exert themselves heroically and find they cannot sleep at night, so wound up have they become. Whatever the level of this hindrance, however, the remedy is the same: try to relax, try to stay calm, try to develop equanimity. It is helpful to keep the mind in the moment as far as possible, and not to let it run off to possible future events. A meditation instructor may assist by asking questions—to which he or she already knows the answer—in order to draw the student's attention to what he is doing.

The last of the five hindrances is sceptical doubt. Practising the meditation correctly, you are certain to experience hours or days when sceptical doubt is a problem. The doubts will be about the Centre, the teacher, the meditation and, not least, about yourself. You will wonder what you are doing here, doing these inane exercises, sitting hour after hour and getting increasingly unsure of things.

Sceptical doubt usually arises because the faculty of investigation has been developed strongly—too strongly for the balance of other positive factors at the time. Starting to see more clearly into things, you become so interested that you generate greater investigation than you need. That investigation sees so many different sides to things that you cannot resolve them; you end up with more questions than you started with.

One way of coping with doubt is to restrain investigation and to have more confidence in the meditative process. This enables you to endure through the difficult patches. If you then ask intelligent questions when you get the opportunity, this can very often settle the doubt.

There is another aspect to sceptical doubt that occurs when a meditator has previously been committed to another way of thinking. In this country, that is usually either Science or the Christian religion, both of which exert a powerful influence on the mind. If there is residual attachment to previous views, it virtually guarantees that the meditator will experience severe doubts about the new way that he or she is practising. In such cases, the best course of action is to be patient, to temporarily put aside reliance on previous views and to practise until the strengths of the new way have been discovered. The Buddha used to suggest an introductory period of at least four months for those coming from other ways and the advice is still valid today. The worst thing to do is try to compare the two approaches; that leads only to doubt and confusion, for their very premises are different.

Through practising right meditation, a meditator identifies the hindrances, learns to overcome them and finally uncovers and learns to recognise purity of mind.

Purity of mind is, in essence, freedom from hindrances. Consequently, it is freedom from wanting things to be different than they are. That does not necessarily mean that there is utter calm, externally and internally, for there may be quite a lot going on. There could be external commotion, for example, and yet the mind can still be free from hindrances. There could be a severe pain in the back, and yet the mind can still be free from hindrances. As each of the five hindrances has an element of craving or hatred within it, when they are suppressed there is at that time no craving or hatred; there is no craving for things to be different.

Temporarily overcoming the hindrances is like being let out of prison or having finally paid off a crushing debt. Suddenly free from its shackles, the mind goes quiet and still and becomes spacious. You feel as though you have all the time in the world and are perfectly contented to be where you are, doing what you are doing. In most cases, the body is also calm, bringing a distinct feeling of well-being.

Purity of mind represents a perfect balance of mental factors.

Mindfulness is good, concentration is good, the effort is right, there is confidence in what you are doing and just the right amount of investigation. No factor is out of balance. None is too strong; none is too weak. Everything is just right.

Meditation does not stop when the hindrances are put aside, however. Indeed, you could say that it has only now properly begun. To continue, we need firstly to be able to observe purity of mind, and to do nothing about it other than keep it in being. This takes a certain amount of restraint, for every so often the craving to do something tries to creep back in. Secondly, we have to deepen the meditation and, here, we are faced with a choice.

Insight meditation develops supramundane wisdom and is developed differently from concentration meditations that emphasise calmness and tranquillity. This is the point at which the practice of the two kinds of meditations diverges.

Calming meditations are dependent upon ever-deepening tranquillity and equanimity, gained through concentration. To become calmer, we have to enhance, to encourage, to develop those very things. To gain tranquillity, we continue to attend to the rise and fall but, in this case, emphasise its repetitive nature, treating it as an ever-present object on which to focus the mind intently. The objective is to gain one-pointedness of mind, concentration on a single focus that will suppress all disturbances and allow entry into deeper states of mind. In essence, we have to stop thinking and start experiencing.

With deepening tranquillity, the mind and body become calmer and calmer. There is much blissful feeling suffusing the whole body, while mindfulness ensures that there is no sloth or torpor. The mind remains bright and alert, though aloof from interest in sensory things, and the calm states of mind are easily maintained. Pursuing the practice of tranquillity, the mind becomes further removed from the hindrances and a 'mark of concentration' arises. Typically, for an individual meditator, this could be a disc or sphere of light that arises at the point of attention, though there are many variations. Transferring attention to the mark, concentration deepens further until, eventually, the mind becomes completely stable. Initial purity of mind is easily upset owing to its nearness to the hindrances, but these deeper states, known as *jhāna*, the fixed meditations, are unshakeable. There are eight different levels, each one more subtle and refined than the previous one. With continued work, we can improve the depth of concentration and the resulting tranquillity.

It is also possible, having developed the first four fixed meditations, to go on to develop what are known as the psychic powers. These include the ability to know the minds of others, to travel in the mental body and things of that nature. The powers are a fascinating field of study, but one that does not particularly concern us as insight meditators, for the whole of the psychic field can be seen as a distraction from the task of generating insight wisdom. We have only so much time and energy. It is worthwhile using them in a way calculated to gain the best long-term advantage. Insight wisdom has the potential to free us forever from suffering. Deep tranquillity and psychic powers, no matter how fascinating, provide only temporary relief.

If we are to deepen the meditation towards the goal of insight, our primary objective is to develop understanding as opposed to tranquillity. To develop understanding requires a great deal of observation and investigation. So, instead of developing calmness beyond that necessary to pay mindful attention, the key here is to develop investigation and observation. As with all successful meditation, this has to be done without haste and without excessive effort; we need to maintain the balance of mental factors experienced in purity of mind. The primary object of the meditation is also different. For insight meditation, we focus upon one of the three marks of all conditioned phenomena. These are transience, unsatisfactoriness and non-self. The most usual mark to choose is that of transience, the rise and fall of things.

The observation of rise and fall with a view to developing tranquillity focuses upon the repetitive experience of breathing without remarking on its transience. Insight meditation, in contrast, is less concerned about the repetition and more interested to note that every experience dies, quickly, and never repeats. Each instance of rise or fall is new, unique and impermanent at any level we can observe. Our primary object is the mark of transience.

The three marks inhere in every single experience, in every conditioned thing or process. Everything of this kind is transient, everything of this kind is unsatisfactory in the sense that we cannot do anything with it because it does not last, and everything whatever, conditioned and unconditioned, is non-self and does not have a discrete central core that we can grasp.

Deepening the meditation towards insight gives us an ever more subtle experience of these three marks and this is often painful, for it brings us in confrontation with our own mistaken ideas. Each new insight challenges some of the treasured notions, ideas and concepts that we have held perhaps for years. If there is clinging, then the fact that our old ideas have to be thrown out in the light of new experience can be painful in the extreme. Insight meditation involves a radical reappraisal of the way we see the world.

With much work and many insights, understanding is won. The mistaken views are corrected, clinging is undermined through the wisdom of experience.

Pursuing the path of meditation, eventually we arrive at a state free from suffering. If we travel the path of concentration, deepening tranquillity, we attain freedom from suffering and clinging that is temporary, being engineered through suppression. Travelling the insight path, craving, clinging and suffering are destroyed, never more to resurface.

Freedom of mind is a common goal and approached in many ways. All of them are successful to a point, allowing some respite from the cares of the workaday world. All but one, however, suffer from the same fault: they are temporary. Temporary solutions to the problem of suffering are legion, including all kinds of diversions and entertainment, and many kinds of escapism.

Many people find temporary freedom of mind through working. Working hard, entranced by the work they are doing, all their cares and troubles drop away. Finding that work is a successful means of overcoming distress, some become workaholics. Other people take to different forms of activity, like sports, for example. They too force concentration upon a single object and cut out the hindrances. The problem lies in the fact that the freedom gained cannot last; the hindrances inevitably arise some time after the activity ceases. Such activities give great calmness but develop little or no understanding. They cannot be relied upon.

Calming meditation is a purer form of the same basic idea: that intense concentration on a single object or process can suppress the hindrances for a considerable length of time. The freedom from clinging that develops ensures suffering cannot arise at that time. The effects are not lasting because the cause of suffering, craving, is put aside only temporarily.

For permanent freedom, we need to look to *vipassanā*, insight meditation. The understanding gained through observation of transience cuts through the roots of craving, cuts through the potentially ever-present hindrances to eradicate and destroy them.

Through insight meditation, we come to know from experience that there is nothing lasting in the world at any level. Whatever we look at, whatever we experience, with whatever sense, there is nothing in the world that lasts. When we know that, by experience, then it is not that we put aside craving, but that we are unable to crave for anything. We cannot cling to something that we know does not last. We can have no longing for something that is present for such a fleeting instant it scarcely exists at all. We do not deliberately choose to stop craving for things; we do not decide to stop wanting things to be different; we find ourselves unable to want things to be different. We know that all experience is constantly in flux and that there is no thing that exists to be different.

If we come to the fullest depth of understanding then there is nothing more to do, for we now see the world in a completely different way. This is not a question of belief or faith. It is rather a question of total internal transformation.

Just this is the end of suffering that marks the goal of the Buddha's path. With the eradication of craving, comes the eradication of all suffering whatever. In the absence of craving, it is not possible to perform actions that lead to rebirth in this or any other realm. We have stepped off the wheel of birth and death, gone beyond *samsāra*, the endless faring on, and rest content in the eternal now.

10

The Real Meaning of Grasping

Grasping and clinging restrict us enormously for we are unable to operate at our true potential if we grasp, if we cling to things. Clinging restricts our opportunities in the present, for we are never really 'here', preferring always to look somewhere else for solace and fulfilment.

In a factory, a worker's sole topic of conversation is his experiences in the army, when he was a young man. In a suburban house, the parents of a dead child have kept her room unchanged for years, as a shrine. A clinging mother will not let go of her grown sons and daughters, trying still to run their lives as if they were children. A lonely, ageing woman has never got over being jilted, fifty years ago.

Clinging does not operate solely on past objects, however; it is just as common to grasp at and cling to an imagined future. A man talks constantly about the book he is going to write, some day. A young woman has her heart set on meeting Mr Right, finding true love and having a marriage ceremony fit for a queen. Many spend hours planning what they might do with their winnings should they eventually win the Lottery. A man poisons his neighbour's small tree because he thinks that in a few years' time it might become tall enough to shade his conservatory.

The future we might cling to does not have to be so far away. A gambler bets everything he has on a throw of the dice or the turn of a card. A meditator strains every fibre trying to achieve his idea of concentration.

Many sports-people are fuelled by a passionate desire to be first, to win. If they allow that passionate desire to dominate, if the final goal is constantly before the mind's eye, then they cannot operate at their full potential. Driven by passion, they exert maximum effort causing the body to tense, movements to become erratic and performance, unpredictable. Indeed, it is well known that peak performance is *not* simply a question of speed, stamina and technique—there are also psychological factors to take into account. The mind has to be focused without being anxious, determined without being tense, pliable yet supremely attentive. The contestant has to be psychologically prepared for battle and has to understand the psychology of personal combat, rather like the martial artist. If these conditions are met, then an athlete's performance improves greatly.

In essence, it is a question of restraining—setting aside for the time being—obsessive grasping at the goal, at the prize. It means, in fact, not to try so hard, to be more relaxed in exercising physical skills. When grasping at the idea of success—with its concomitant fear of failure—is removed from the mind, the resulting poise makes it possible for the sprinter to shave a few vital split seconds off his time, for the tennis player to improve her service both in power and accuracy, for the discus-thrower to get a few extra centimetres on his best throw.

Grasping is detrimental in any area of human endeavour. Wherever there is excessive personal attachment to or identification with an ideal, there is grasping that is ruinous to health and mental balance.

Some people, for instance, try to insure themselves against any conceivable eventuality. The net result is that all spare cash is taken up by payment of premiums, leaving none for normal enjoyments, and there is constant awareness of potential danger from all sides. Grasping excessively at the idea of security, life becomes a prison.

Others, in complete contrast, grasp more strongly at enjoyment in the present, spending all their hard-earned wages on entertainment and enjoyment. Often borrowing to satisfy their desires, they constantly juggle their debts, getting deeper and deeper into trouble until they run out of friends or have to declare bankruptcy.

Some take as their ideal the perfect relationship—constant, loving, eternal. But relationships, even 'perfect' ones, break down. What then? With excessive grasping there is a definite tendency to refuse to recognise signs of disharmony or breakdown and, when it does finally become unavoidable, the suffering is immense.

A woman described her husband as a brute who would never speak to her unless to criticise or to complain. She came to believe that she could be happy only if they separated. The trouble was that she also believed that she could be happy only with the material support his income provided. She was convinced she could not live with him and convinced she could not live without him. Trapped between the two conflicting desires, her confusion produced total stasis; she could do nothing.

If she had been able to restrain the grasping after security, or the grasping after freedom—one or the other, a number of possibilities would have become immediately apparent. She could have left her husband and accepted living in reduced circumstances until she made a new life for herself. She could have sought formal divorce with maintenance payments. She could have stayed and lived her own life, seeking fulfilment in activities outside the home. She could have accepted her difficult circumstances and tried to learn from them.

In any failed or failing relationship, there are innumerable opportunities. If one of the parties is prepared to let go of a previously entrenched opinion then a great deal can be done. If both parties are prepared to let go of their entrenched opinions, then it is possible to build something wonderful out of the wreckage. It all depends on letting go, on controlling the grasping after the things you believe you want above all else.

The folly of refusing to let go can also show itself in the commercial world, especially in times of recession. A man spent years building up a successful company. Recession came along, orders fell off and the continued prosperity of the business came under serious threat. He retrenched, made a few token redundancies, dug in and prepared to wait out the recession. He kept on telling everybody that everything would be fine if only they could get that one big order; they would not have to close the factory, they could keep everything going. He drove his sales force unmercifully. They responded with enthusiasm and did indeed get some orders, but the recession deepened and, not having bottomless capital reserves, he was eventually forced into receivership, into bankruptcy. He lost everything.

He had resolutely ignored changing conditions, and had grasped at, clung to, his vision of the successful business he had built up. In consequence, he lost the lot. Had he heeded the signs, matters could have turned out very differently. He could perhaps have sold up, even at a loss, and salvaged a substantial part of what he had worked so hard for over the years. He could have shut down, laid everyone off and waited for the economic tides to turn.

Hindsight is, of course, a dubious counsellor, but signs of imminent disaster are nearly always available if we are clear-sighted enough to observe them and, perhaps more importantly, to act on them. The trouble is that much of the time such indicators are obscured by grasping. Refusing to contemplate loss and grasping at continued success ensures that we ignore portents of disaster.

One sure way to success in any field, given adequate skill and hard work, is in fact to remove grasping or at least suppress it for the time being. This allows us to maximise our potential in almost any area of endeavour. Restraint of grasping is a difficult task that needs great attention to mental detail and an ability to change mental behaviour patterns. When approached properly, however, successful restraint brings great rewards.

Another area of human activity that suffers when grasping is present is communication; any breakdown of communication—and the battles that ensue—is always due to grasping. Say, for example, someone asks his manager for a pay rise. So concerned is he about the outcome of the interview, so strongly does he grasp at the idea of success (or failure), that he can hardly talk. His request rejected, he knows that he has not presented his case well and feels that he has let himself down. Falling into self-hatred, he decides that, if trying to get more money is going to be so painful, he is probably better off without it.

Grasping cripples us in so many different ways. Removing grasping is the single most effective way of unlocking our potential. It is not that new opportunities are created—not at all; it is simply that opportunities already in existence are seen and can be acted upon. Nowhere is this truer than in meditation. In meditation, the understanding of grasping is crucial to progress.

In meditation, the first steps are all based on the control of personal behaviour, initially by way of the precepts. Some people do not find it a problem—they already live in conformity with the precepts. Others have difficulty with an established habit that is not in keeping with the spirit of restraint that the precepts embody. For instance, there may be a problem with habitual drinking that is difficult to bring under control. With effort, with perseverance and sufficient motivation, such obstacles can always be overcome. It then becomes obvious that the stumbling block was not the drinking as such—the real problem was grasping at certain patterns of behaviour and being unable, because unwilling, to let go of them. Whether the difficulty is obvious—like breaking one of the precepts—or more elusive—like over-effort in the meditation practice, it is always due to grasping at habitual behaviour patterns.

Once past the early stages of meditation, restraint requires greater subtlety. Every meditator is enjoined to practise sense-restraint, to try to control attachment to and grasping at the sense of sight, the sense of hearing and so on. Further, there is emphasis on keeping the attention in the moment, trying always to come back to what is happening here and now. All this depends on the restraint of grasping at habitual mental activities.

At this intermediate stage, meditation is often plagued by the five hindrances. Analysing the practice carefully, however, it is apparent that, rather than five, there really are only two major obstacles. Whether one is practising *samatha* (that is, concentration and calming) or insight meditation, the two fundamental obstacles are excitement and laziness. These, when examined closely, turn out to be dependent on grasping.

All of us are familiar with both excitement and laziness and, with some thought, can usually see how they arise. Excitement, for instance, arises either from efforts to grasp an objective or from anticipation, from grasping at the *idea* of a future event. Laziness, on the other hand, comes from attachment to and grasping at comfort and pleasant feeling, or from unwillingness to work at restraint.

Before meditation proper can begin it is essential to establish some tranquillity. Ideally, both body and mind should be calm and relaxed for, if the meditator ignores one or the other, the calmness produced is unbalanced and the meditation cannot develop properly. For example, the individual who has a tendency towards being over-energetic will often find that the body is tense and agitated, painful and stiff. With some effort, the mind may become moderately calm but the body can remain distressed—and that is sufficient to prevent the meditation from getting any deeper. In contrast, a meditator who has a tendency to grasp at pleasure and comfort finds that the body is wonderfully calm and relaxed but that the mind wanders into daydream or even sleep and cannot be made to settle to any disciplined observation. In this case, the mind needs energising, waking up, for the daydreaming is not tranquillity but rather inattention.

Neither of these states is alert, neither is bright and clear; in fact, both are rather dull. Both kinds of people, the energetic and the lazy, suffer from very similar problems of unbalanced tranquillity. In each case the imbalance is due to inappropriate levels of effort and reflects a lack of skill at this level of the meditation. This wrong balance is a common difficulty for many setting out on their meditative career and, if not properly addressed, can persist for a surprisingly long time. It is definitely worth taking the trouble to correct this wrong concentration as early as possible.

It is entirely possible to balance the mind rightly so that all tensions and dullness can disappear. To bring this about, we must know four things. We have to know what wrong concentration is, how it arises, its disadvantages and the escape from it.

What is wrong concentration? It is a blend of craving, of effort and intense concentration itself. Its objective is to produce some kind of desired result *in the shortest possible time*. Now that desired result need not be so exalted as enlightenment or even deep concentration. It may be simply the wish to do the meditation well, to succeed in that more limited sense. The desire may simply be to remove the pain and discomfort that has currently arisen. The desire may be to avoid disturbances that are thought to be due to noise or some kind of external intrusion. There is always a desire to do the meditation rightly, immediately, here and now, and to get past a perceived problem.

When such ambition is not acknowledged and restrained, the next step in the sequence of events is to attempt to achieve the objective. Typically, this involves narrowing the focus of mind and then pouring every ounce of energy you possess into that small point while resolutely fending off anything that looks as if it may distract you from the task.

Depending on the exact circumstances, there arises one of several different results. The mind and body become rigid and unworkable. The mind gets calmer but is dazed and cloudy with a vague awareness of body tension. The body may relax but the mind becomes day-dreamy and unable to hold its attention on anything. The meditator may initially become very calm but then slip into a vivid but fantastical dream-state. There may be a band of pressure around the head, intense headaches, neck tension and pains in the shoulders and back.

For those new to meditation, the mind often seems calm even under these conditions of imbalance, but this is so only because there is at that time no knowledge of true tranquillity. True tranquillity is a very different matter, as we shall see in a moment.

Wrong concentration arises out of a determination to succeed coupled with a lack of skill in directing the mind. We know that worldly success often can be gained by working passionately towards a goal. We know that extremes of craving—or hatred—work to produce what we want, although we may not use these terms. If we get passionately involved, pour all our efforts into achieving results, we know it is possible to bring about sometimes-remarkable success. We are conditioned to expect great efforts to produce great results.

Not surprisingly, we apply the same principles to the meditation and so convinced are we of the benefits of this extreme kind of endeavour that some of us are reluctant to give it up; we cling to it. Someone with this characteristic does not give up easily. At the slightest sign of success, his heart starts pounding, his mouth goes dry and he is on tenterhooks waiting for the success he believes is just round the corner. When things are not going well, instead of easing off he re-doubles his efforts and forces the pace even more. This course of action, far from bringing success, often ends in total despair and self-hatred at his inability to succeed.

What are the disadvantages of wrong concentration? The simplest answer is that it does not work. It will sometimes produce a superficial calm, as often as not it will produce pain. What it does produce in every case without fail is dullness of mind—and with that, true meditation is impossible.

Some would-be meditators claim that wrong concentration 'just happens' and there is, therefore, nothing they can do about it. Experienced meditators know, from having seen the arising of wrong concentration very clearly, that it is in fact something we choose to do. At first, though, it is very difficult to distinguish the choice we make. Excessive effort has become so habitual that we are not aware of the habit in operation. Before the problem can be overcome, we have to become more mindful of our mental actions.

There are tendencies to behaviour and there are actual actions. Many people have developed a tendency towards wrong concentration. The tendency predisposes the mind to act in a certain way. It is not action itself; it just, as it were, opens a door through which you could go if you wished. The action is not inevitable; it can be restrained. You do not have to go ahead.

A tendency arises whether you like it or not; there is nothing whatever you can do about it because it is a result of past actions. The next step in the process, however, is for action itself to be initiated— and that you *can* do something about. You can choose to act, or you can choose not to act. If you choose to restrain your previously habitual action, you have for the time being conquered wrong concentration. To do this, you have to be extremely alert; you have to see the difference between the tendency and the activity itself.

With strong mindfulness, it is possible to see how the choice is made. It is a little like walking down a corridor with open doorways at intervals on both sides. Above each door is a legend indicating the name of the room beyond. A quick glance at some of them is instructive: you see 'ill will', 'effort', 'craving', 'flurry and worry' and several others. Due to past conditioning, you find yourself strongly drawn to, say, the one marked 'effort'. Through the opening, you can see the territory you would enter were you to go through the door. The temptation is very strong—especially if you have been conditioned to believe great effort is a desirable and effective means to an end—but you do not have to go in; you can resist and, in resisting, stay mindful and self-possessed. Of course, often we are insufficiently alert and, through habit, go through, whereupon we find ourselves in all kinds of difficulty. While it is possible to go into reverse and get out, it is much more difficult than refusing to enter in the first place.

Something that may help to overcome wrong concentration that has arisen (you have gone through the door and find yourself in difficulties) is to take to heart the Parable of the Saw. The Buddha said, 'Even if bandits should capture you and saw you limb from limb with a two-handled saw, if any one of you should allow hatred to arise in your mind on that account, you are no doers of my teaching.' Pain and discomfort, however brought about, are not sufficient reason for hatred and actions based on it; they can be accepted without resistance.

To most, not to resist distress seems difficult, perhaps even impossible, but the parable contains a valuable lesson. If you can come willingly to accept the pains, the discomforts, the obstacles you run into in the meditation practice, you are in fact halfway home. It is possible to overcome wrong concentration completely by willing acceptance of discomfort. Indeed, it is possible to overcome any of the hindrances with willing acceptance. It is not easy, but it works wonderfully well. Then you begin to understand true tranquillity.

When acceptance is mastered, a meditator is able easily to avoid the passionate response to thoughts of success and failure in the meditation. When the mind remains calm no matter what is going on, then it also becomes luminously clear. This state is completely different from the false tranquillity that accompanies some types of wrong concentration. The mind is tranquil and the body is tranquil—which allows for sustained meditation of a depth and subtlety previously unattainable. Meditations become delightful, something to look forward to. When this stage is reached, meditation is something you truly enjoy and would not miss for the world.

Meditators habituated to over-effort will still have a bias towards using mental blasting techniques; the conditioned tendency is not eradicated easily and will still arise from time to time. Should habitual over-effort be employed, however, it is obvious what has happened and the meditator will know what to do—or what not to do—to overcome it. He will know the escape from the problem.

By restraining wrong concentration, by true acceptance and by mastering the passionate response, it is possible to come to true tranquillity. That tranquillity is an essential precursor of the real business of meditation. Whether developing *samatha* (calming meditation) or *vipassanā* (insight meditation), now is the time to introduce the meditation subject proper.

It is at this point that the two kinds of meditation practices diverge: calming meditation is developed by emphasising tranquillity, insight by emphasising attention to the mark of transience.

The way of *samatha* or calming meditation is based on control, on the masterful restraint of grasping itself. We need to learn to control grasping to an even more subtle degree than we have so far managed. With great mindfulness and deep concentration, exquisite control will bring freedom of mind greater and more delightful than anything experienced so far.

While concentration allows you to destroy all obstacles to tranquillity in the short term, the roots of grasping are still firmly embedded in the mind and are unaffected. They still have the potential to throw up new growth, new grasping, at any time. The way of control removes suffering to a distance and, with continued vigilance, keeps it at bay. The future is in no way assured, though, for the old problems with grasping will occur again, given the right conditions. No matter how delightful, no amount of calming meditation can eradicate the roots of behaviour that give rise to suffering.

In contrast, the way of vision, the way of insight, does not depend upon control in the same manner.

Within the tranquillity already developed by control, by overcoming wrong concentration, the passionate response and the hindrances, the *vipassanā* meditator cultivates an attitude of enquiry that leads eventually to a transmutation of view. The way of vision brings the meditator to see things differently than he has before, brings personal and undeniable proof that things are indeed transient, unsatisfactory and non-self.

The roots of grasping grow only in the soil of ignorance. What ignorance? Ignorance of reality itself, of the four noble truths, of the three marks of existence; ignorance of the fact that all the things you treasure are like so many soap bubbles, ephemeral. Such ignorance leads you to grasp and grasp again—and then you suffer as the bubbles burst all around you.

As understanding grows, grasping diminishes, for it becomes more apparent that things do not last long enough for the grasping to be effective. The only product of seizing on and clinging to things is frustration and unhappiness, suffering. Eventually, insight develops to the point that all things are known to be transient, unsatisfactory and non-self. When this level of development is reached, grasping dies away and, with it, the three roots of ignorance, craving and hatred.

The roots of grasping are dug out, are totally removed, only by *insight*. Insight is experiential understanding gained from contemplation of the transience of all conditioned things. Unless that understanding arises, the roots remain untouched and potentially very dangerous.

In overview, the meditator changes from always seeking his own advantage and becomes far less self-centred. This change comes about dependent upon recognition, through the meditation practice, of at least two essential facts. The first is that all things arise dependent upon other things. For instance, you can only experience a feeling if there is preceding contact with a sense-object. Similarly, distress, anguish, can arise only if there is preceding grasping; if there were no grasping, there would be no distress. The second essential is that the meditator has to experience the three marks: that everything is transient, everything is unsatisfactory and everything is non-self and therefore uncontrollable.

The change in a meditator's outlook comes about from experience of these facts through meditation; it is not due merely to study and intellectual knowledge nor does it come from analysis of the past. We are not in the least bit interested in whether we were unloved as children, whether we suffered some specific trauma earlier in this life or in some previous one. We are not at all interested in the historical origins of our emotional states. All we need to see—in the new, tranquil state that arises with the overcoming of wrong concentration and the hindrances—is the conditioned arising of states and the three marks of transience, unsatisfactoriness and non-self.

* * *

There are three 'doors to deliverance', doors to enlightenment, one for each of the marks. If in our meditation practice we pay particular attention to the mark of transience, we are aiming for the door that leads to the signless liberation. We see that all things change, that nothing lasts, that all things are in fact disappearing like bubbles ceaselessly bursting.

We might choose to pay attention to the mark of suffering. We see that anything we might grasp at is actually unsatisfactory; it does not give us what we want; it turns to ashes, as it were, immediately. Doing this, we aim for what is known as the desireless liberation—desireless because it is impossible to desire something we know to be completely unsatisfactory.

We might choose to look at non-self, recognising that this whole body-mind carries on without the necessity of an ego, without 'me' being necessary at all. It is probably the finest redundancy in the world, to realise that the self is an irrelevancy and that it does not exist in any permanent fashion. Life goes on without self, and no one needs to be holding the reins all the time. In this case, we aim for the void liberation, the liberation based on seeing that all phenomena are void of self or what pertains to self.

These are the three gateways to liberation and, aiming at any of these, we see clearly why great force can never produce success in the meditation practice. Excessive effort unbalances the mind and body, rendering them unable to sustain the depth of tranquillity needed for insight to develop. There is also the major obstacle of the craving, the desire, behind the effort. It is the craving, the grasping at success, that produces the frustration and the suffering. The process is circular, with no beginning and no ending. Every time we grasp, we create suffering; every time we react against suffering, we grasp ignorantly at something else. We work hard merely to maintain this particularly vicious circle until, through the development of sufficient mindfulness to allow restraint, we see what we are doing.

Through increasing mindfulness and clear comprehension, it becomes obvious that, whenever we ignore the three marks, we suffer. With this realisation, it is clear that the only way to deal with the whole problem of suffering is to pay exquisitely careful attention to all mental and physical processes, not just the ones we think are 'best' or most appropriate.

Using *vipassanā* meditation, we begin to get glimpses of what ultimate freedom must be like. Attending to the three marks—and understanding conditioning—it is possible to remove completely not only grasping but the very roots of grasping. Using the way of vision, insight, we dig up the roots, shred them, burn them and scatter the ash so that never again under any circumstances can the roots generate new growth. The roots of suffering might never have existed and will never arise again.

'*Vipassanā* is,' the Buddha said, 'the one way to the eradication of grasping.' Control is good, but it is not enough: right concentration brings tangible mundane benefits but, of itself, it can never eliminate suffering for all time. Wrong concentration does not even have the distinction of providing benefits and will never get you to the other shore, not in a million years, no matter how hard you try. The only way to overcome grasping and clinging is to remove the passionate response. This must be done not only superficially, by way of control, but by digging out and destroying its very roots with understanding, with insight, with perception of the three marks.

The successful meditator is then capable of realising his or her fullest potential, whatever that may be. Having gone beyond the world, he finds, paradoxically, that he can then act in the world more effectively than before. Having removed the grasping at success that attended every previous effort, there is no longer any attachment to the results of actions. With the mind clear of obstacles, he can now operate at his maximum possible potential. Anyone in this position may of course need training in this or that mundane skill but can learn at his most effective speed due to the absence of grasping and attachment.

Truly, the way to happiness—whether the happiness in the world or the highest happiness beyond it—is to eradicate grasping. The eradication of grasping is possible only if you find out what grasping really means and come to understand all its devious ways. Knowing the source of suffering you can eliminate it through skill and understanding, through the path of *vipassanā* meditation.

11

The Burden of Meditation

We sometimes find it hard to believe, but other people do not necessarily see the world in the same way that we do. All of us have a tendency to project our own views and outlooks on the people whom we meet, and yet we are in fact very different from one another.

Once, in Greece, I met two people who were island-hopping and had just missed the ferry to the next island. One of them was devastated by their misfortune: they were not going to get to see the next island; their entire schedule, their entire holiday, was upset. The other was delighted: now they could spend more time on this island and really get to know the people.

One young man, about twenty or so, makes what he truly believes to be 'the best omelette in the world', and is very proud of his skill. A woman who is in fact a first-class cook believes her skills are deficient and, lacking confidence, she would not dream of giving a dinner party or cooking a meal for someone she did not know very well.

Many people love classical music but some young people dismiss such music as outdated. They far prefer acid-house music, hip-hop or rap—all of it at a volume that seems life-threatening.

We are very different. Each of us is unique, although just how unique we often do not realise. But, though we are different, there are of course many similarities. We can describe people by the ways they behave, by the kinds of jobs they do, by their basic mental characteristics. Forms of character analysis are legion. Popular variations include astrological types, introvert/extrovert, aggressive/passive, masculine/feminine and type-A/type-B.

Character analysis is scarcely new; the Buddha defined many classes of people and classes of behaviour. He would say, for instance,

'There are three kinds of people: those who are untrained, those who are undergoing training and those who train no longer.' He also distinguished Dhamma-enthusiasts from meditation-enthusiasts.

Dhamma-enthusiasts had a heavy bias towards the intellectual side of the teaching. They studied assiduously, spent hour upon hour in learned discussion and debate and had little time or inclination for meditation. They gained degrees and qualifications, or their equivalents, all the time extending their grasp of the words, often in more than one language, gaining greater and greater understanding of how the teaching fits together.

Meditation-enthusiasts in complete contrast believed that the answer lay entirely in the meditation. They spent hours and hours in solitary meditation, often in the depths of the forest or the jungle. Developing great skills of concentration, they learned to pierce the veils that divide us from other realms and other beings, and to develop personal insight to a depth that those untrained could scarcely begin to comprehend.

There was often intense rivalry between the two groups. The scholars would criticise and belittle meditators as ignorant, unlettered children who were concerned only to escape from what they saw as the real world. Meditators criticised their bookish brothers, who did not know tranquillity from tension or equanimity from indifference. They could define the words, of course, but they did not know directly the experience the words described.

Each group would occasionally complain of the other to the Buddha. The scholars said that it was foolish to spend so much time in meditation and never be able to expound or explain the teaching to another. Meditators expressed their concern that to focus on intellectual knowledge alone would cut the real heart out of the teaching, so that it would become as dry as dust and blow away on the winds of time.

The Buddha was adamant that both approaches were vitally necessary to the overall health of the teaching. He instructed each group to honour the other, for each was doing 'that which is hard to do'. Study is a burden; meditation is a burden.

The terms have never been lost. Ordaining as a monk in the East, one has to choose between shouldering the burden of the books or the burden of meditation. Tonight I want to talk to you about the burden of meditation.

★ ★ ★

The burden of meditation is to dedicate your life, whatever your circumstances, to gaining eventual success in the practice of meditation. There are two kinds of success: success in concentration and success in insight.

Meditation is a burden because, to practise it, we have to go against our natural inclinations. We have to restrain some kinds of behaviour and encourage others. We have to set aside time—sometimes out of a busy schedule and often with every fibre of our being suggesting that perhaps we could miss it just this once. Meditation is difficult. It is difficult to get started and difficult to maintain until real progress has been made. It needs a great deal of work and sacrifice.

In the light of these difficulties, we need to make the most of our efforts. To make the most effective use of the work we put in, we need to enlist the power of habit and routine in our fight against apathy and temptation. We need also to recognise the power of action: some actions lead away from the path, some assist greatly— more of which later.

There is also the vexed question of friends, especially for the person new to meditation. Often someone comes along to meditation from a group of people who regularly drink alcohol or take drugs and are devoted to the pursuit of pleasure and indulgence at every opportunity. The new meditator tries hard to refrain from these excesses but finds it extremely difficult in the company of his friends who have other ideas.

If he persists in his meditation, it is usual to find that he begins to pull away—not so much from his friends as from the activities they enjoy. In short, their paths through life begin to diverge too much for the friendship to continue as it was before. This can be difficult, for it means leaving something familiar without any guarantees of success in the future.

★ ★ ★

The Buddha defined four kinds of progress on the spiritual path and, thereby, four kinds of people. There are those who travel the path quickly and with ease, those who go quickly but with difficulty, those who go slowly with ease and those who go slowly and with difficulty.

Why do these differences exist? Why are people so diverse? The differences depend upon two things: past conditioning through the actions one has performed, and the current environment. Through inclination, each of us chooses a path in life. With hard work and the right opportunities, an individual may choose to become a musician, a scientist, a thief, a banker, a cook, a soldier, an assassin, a spy, an engineer, a housewife, a dress-designer or an accountant. He or she might choose to be rich or poor, a monk or a nun, a sailor, a racing-driver, a drunkard. The list is endless.

Such lifestyles in the past, and in the present, develop completely different ways of perceiving the world, as well as different skills and abilities. These all have a bearing when it comes to the practice of meditation.

Someone who has been a long-term drunkard in the past—not necessarily in a past life, but perhaps in the past of this one—will have a tendency towards confusion. Someone who takes drugs or has taken drugs a lot often has a marked tendency towards living in fantasies of his own creation. Someone who has indulged a strong tendency to laziness in the past has a tendency towards sloth and torpor in the present. Someone who has been skilled at exerting effort in the past, has never let an obstacle stand in his way, is likely to be very energetic but also to suffer from agitation.

Habitual tendencies are not all bad, of course. Someone who has developed loving-kindness in the past is likely to be full of confidence and faith now. Someone who has done a great deal of study is likely to have well-developed intellectual faculties. Someone who has exercised discrimination—that is, looked at life, pondered on it, thought about it—is likely to be wiser than someone who has not. Someone who has used will-power a lot tends to be very decisive.

A mixture of such skills and abilities conditions our personal progress on the path, whether it is fast and with ease or slow, with difficulty.

Buddhism is full of lists, and I cannot resist saying that these four kinds of progress depend upon three other kinds of progress: progress in mundane behaviour, progress in concentration and progress in insight. Progress, or lack of it, in these areas is most obvious to a trained meditation instructor, and a meditator's account of his practice often says more about the meditator than the meditation, as the following examples illustrate.

In a meditation interview, someone might say that things are 'falling apart' and that there really is not much progress at all. To the trained eye, however, it is obvious that the meditator is seeing things with much greater clarity than ever before. His perception is sharp and he knows what is going on; he is much more mindful. The meditation might be difficult, but there is certainly great improvement. He is indeed making progress, much as he thinks otherwise.

Another person may claim to be experiencing great peace, and yet sit there with his shoulders up round his ears, twisting his fingers together and crossing and uncrossing his legs. Seeing the obvious signs of agitation and lack of calmness, the instructor knows that the individual is putting a brave face on a difficult situation and will usually offer advice on calming and relaxation.

Another claims to have followed instructions religiously, but has made no progress whatever. There is only one possible conclusion: he cannot have followed instruction, no matter what he thinks. Systematic application in the right way cannot fail; it must produce results. If the results do not appear, the meditator is unwittingly—or, on occasion, deliberately—failing to work in the suggested way.

★ ★ ★

What progress is realistically possible for the average meditator?

Let us look first at success in the world, mundane progress. Here we are talking about progress towards the ending—or at least the reduction—of suffering in the world. This has little or nothing to do with the acquisition of wealth and status so sought after by many. It is rather to learn to accept the way the world actually operates, and to bring our views and behaviour in line with natural laws.

Progress in the mundane sphere is dependent entirely upon clear comprehension, or right view, and applied effort. At this stage, mundane right view specifically means adopting and trying to live by the following five views. They are 'right' because they accurately reflect the true facts of life.

The first is, 'There is action and result.' Every action we do with craving or hatred (or with loving-kindness or compassion) will have a result. Selfish actions have unpleasant results; unselfish actions have pleasant ones. To adopt this view as your own means that you accept responsibility for your own circumstances, inner and outer. It has far-reaching consequences, for you realise that the present is the outcome of the past, and that you can affect your future welfare by actions here and now.

In a similar vein, 'There is result of giving.' It is very definitely worthwhile to be generous; it pays off on a personal level. This is intelligent self-interest: this kind of action harms no one at all and is of benefit to both oneself and others.

'There are mother and father.' This cryptic, mundane truth seems self-evident—of course there are mother and father: we would not be here otherwise. But the point here is that because one's parents gave one birth into this human realm, from which it is possible to reach enlightenment itself, they are due great respect. The Buddha said that, even if you should carry your mother and father one on each shoulder for the rest of your life, you could never repay the debt you owe them.

'There are spontaneously arisen beings.' There are beings who come to birth without parents; they spring into being fully formed with all faculties. This refers to those on other levels of existence who are normally invisible to us in the world of gross materiality. It points to the existence of other worlds, other planes of being, in which one can take birth after death in the material world.

The last of the five points of mundane right view is, 'There are teachers who know these other worlds and who can show the way there.' Such teachers are worthy of respect for that knowledge, for through it they can show us the way to the best possible happiness within the three worlds of *samsāra*.

The five points of right view are critically important because they lead us to adopt a number of significant types of behaviour—notably keeping the precepts and restraining indulgence and selfish action in all areas of activity. The benefits of mundane clear comprehension, or mundane right view, expressed in self-control by the precepts, are harmlessness and a developing concern for other people, often in the form of loving-kindness meditation.

Keeping the precepts and restraining indulgence lead to the elimination of what the Buddha graphically called 'the five guilty dreads'. The five guilty dreads are the fear of being found out in some kind of wrongdoing—theft, murder, wrongful sexual activity, character defamation through gossip or degradation through addiction to alcohol or drugs. Elimination of the five guilty dreads leads to peace of mind, for one knows with certainty that one has nothing to fear; one's mind, one's conduct, is completely pure and one could stand up anywhere and say so.

Note that fearlessness is not at all the same thing as bravery. Bravery is to fear harm but to proceed anyway. Nowhere is bravery more needed than in confronting one's own inner demons and tackling the selfishness that they represent by acceptance and restraint. Fearlessness, in contrast, is having nothing to hide; it results from having overcome some of one's inner demons.

Consideration for others leads to a reduction in self-importance and the development of joyful service to other people. It also leads to greater peace and harmony in communities, small or large, and to greater happiness in the world as a whole.

None of this is possible without at least rudimentary mindfulness. We have to be sufficiently mindful to be aware of our own behaviour patterns. We cannot adjust things if we do not know what we do.

After death, the benefits of mundane right view and the consequent actions continue in the form of rebirth in fortunate planes of existence, where life is considerably easier than here.

* * *

Mundane progress towards freedom from suffering can be enhanced by the practice of concentration meditation. This brings greater refinement and subtlety to the mind and removes, temporarily, the troubles that afflict even the most delightful results obtainable from simple adjustment of physical behaviour.

The essence of concentration is withdrawal of attention from the physical world—in other words, from the five physical senses—while remaining completely alert and conscious. To bring this about, the essential components are sense-restraint and mindfulness. Sense-restraint is not possible without a foundation of self-discipline—which means keeping the precepts at the very least—or the mind is too agitated, too unsettled, through guilt and general indulgence and cannot quieten enough to concentrate. We need mindfulness of sensory and mental processes to an extremely high degree for, as mental behaviour is so much subtler than physical action, we would otherwise be unable to control it.

There are significant markers in the development of concentration and mindfulness. For instance, as you progress, you become aware of your intentions and the subsequent actions. You become aware that, before you change a posture—say from sitting to standing—there has first to be an intention. If there is no intention, there is no change of posture. Before you start walking, there has to be an intention. Before you fall asleep, in most cases there has to be an intention. Before you speak, there has to be an intention. Intention precedes any action, whether physical, mental or verbal. Even to think about something, there has to be an intention. All of these become clear.

Another indicator is the capacity to control mental reactions, in the sense of controlling hindrances at will and overcoming elation and depression. Depression is always preceded by an intention. It takes a great deal of work to stay depressed, and any meditator who has advanced sufficiently will totally conquer his or her depression. Mindfulness and concentration, when properly developed, confer the ability to control the mind to a degree undreamed of by the untrained.

Another mark of progress toward concentration is that a *nimitta* may arise. This may take the form of a pinpoint, disc or sphere of light in the mind (though there are many variations). Another is the occurrence of states of fixed meditation, where the mind is deeply calm, concentrated and unshakeable.

With increasing mindfulness and concentration, you develop the ability to control what you think. If you find the mind running off on a track that you are not happy with, you simply stop it. You see the intention and the following action; you see the effort made to persist with the line of thinking and simply refuse to continue. You stop making the repeated intentions and thereby stop putting effort into the train of thought, which then ceases. Conversely, it is possible to engender happy states of mind at will, by deciding to do so. You can control what you think.

Last, but not least, there is the possibility of developing psychic powers. These alluring developments often occur unbidden and apparently at random to start with. The appearance of strange visions and perceptions can be so interesting that the meditator may get drawn away from his proper focus into areas of mental experience that take up much time and effort, often to the detriment of his overall progress. While proficiency in the psychic powers can certainly be developed—to good effect if you have both the time and suitable circumstances—most people are best advised to treat them with great caution or disregard them altogether.

What are the benefits of concentration and mindfulness? Essentially, there are three.

The first benefit of concentration practised as a calming exercise is the experience of great peace and bliss in the meditation. Additionally, strong residual traces of these delightful mental states carry over into everyday life. At this time, the only complaint about meditations is that they seem too short. An hour passes in what seems like five or ten minutes; a two-hour meditation seems to go by almost as quickly. You get up from the meditation feeling refreshed, calm, happy and looking forward to the next one.

The second benefit of concentration and mindfulness can be the supernormal powers, though, as I said, these are not for everybody, and very much depend on past training and having the right present supporting circumstances. Supernormal powers include creating a mental body in the exact image of the physical and, with consciousness established in that body, being able to become many or single, visible or invisible; able to go in that body through walls, swim in the earth or walk on water. It really is not very difficult, given that we are talking about a mental body that has all of the skills and abilities that you could dream up. I use the word 'dream' quite deliberately here, for the kinds of powers you might experience in a dream-body are the sorts of things you can bring under deliberate control with supernormal powers.

The other psychic powers are the ability to see and hear things at a distance, knowledge of the minds of others, recollection of past lives and the ability to see the death and rebirth of beings from one level to another in dependence on their deeds. These confer understanding of *saṃsāra* and the law of *kamma* in a direct and unmistakable way.

The third and most important benefit of concentration and mindfulness is the development of the capacity to destroy, through insight, the cankers of craving, hatred and ignorance—thus to come to the complete cessation of suffering. This benefit is so important that it demands to be expanded at some length.

* * *

Success in insight—the third benefit of concentration and mindfulness—is supramundane progress, progress that leads beyond the relative world. To develop insight is to develop awareness of the complete transience of all conditioned mental and physical phenomena, without exception. It is to develop clear understanding and direct perception of their unsatisfactory and non-self nature. Ultimately, insight leads to the abandoning of all relative things to abide in *nibbāna*, the beyond.

The entire path to the cessation of anguish depends upon mindfulness and the observation of rise and fall, transience, together with sufficient concentration to allay the hindrances during meditation. It seems too simple for many, but is extremely powerful in its simplicity.

Briefly, insight leads to a weakening of the fetters that bind one to this world and to rebirth in it. It lessens craving and hatred, or attachment, and thus suffering. Ultimately, insight eradicates suffering altogether. This is the goal of all living beings, whether they have defined it clearly or not.

Once the basics have been mastered, each meditator progresses through clearly defined stages.

The first major step is overcoming doubt. The meditator becomes aware of the entirely conditioned nature of action and result, aware of the entirely conditioned nature of mind and body, and realises that in this whole complex of mind and body there is nothing that can be called a self. It is all *anattā*, non-self; it is all conditioned and conditioning. At this point questions tend to fall away to some extent and, with them, the sceptical doubts that often beset the beginner.

The next significant point is 'knowledge of arising and passing away', where you see the rise and fall of mental and physical events with great clarity. You feel that at last you have reached the perfection of meditation. Mindfulness is strong and keen. Everything you observe is seen clearly and precisely. The meditation is calm, bright and alert. This stage of the practice is such a radical change from what went before that some people mistakenly think it is enlightenment itself.

Contributing to the delight of 'arising and passing away' are the strong faith and confidence in the teaching that arise. Indeed, these are so strong that many meditators want to convert everybody they meet. Realising that they have found a teaching that is wonderfully effective, they want to tell everyone about it.

It is here, too, that many of the so-called corruptions of insight arise. There might be bright lights in the mind, tremendous depth of calmness, extremely fine mindfulness. The meditator may become very attached to any or all of these, to the extent that he refuses to move on; and yet, if progress is to be made, move on he must.

When he does finally let go, he moves into areas of experience that are distinctly less pleasant: the knowledges of dissolution, fear, misery and disgust. These traditional terms give some idea of just how difficult these following stages can be, and yet they are essential and unavoidable.

Through closely examining the transience of all mental and physical events it becomes apparent that there is nothing in the world that is capable of providing lasting happiness and satisfaction. Everything begins to look dull, dingy and a waste of time. Just to maintain life is difficult, and happiness, in any lasting sense, seems impossible to find. As the saying has it, 'It's a hard life, and then you die.' It can be extremely trying. Those under instruction are told, if they have not seen it for themselves, that their discomfort is not due to lifestyle or personal failure, as some wrongly suspect, but rather is a meditative experience that should simply be noted as 'not me' and 'not mine'. If the meditator does this, the experience becomes bearable and even interesting. In contrast, those who try to struggle by on their own can have much more difficulty, sometimes pro-longing the agony for a considerable time.

After the experiences of dissolution, fear, misery and disgust there comes—perhaps not surprisingly—'desire for deliverance'. There arises a burning desire to escape the mind-numbing drudgery and futility of the relative world. Try as you might, you can see no way out except through more meditation. You apply yourself again, as though starting at the beginning, to re-observation of the three marks, of the rise and fall of all material and mental experiences. There is great determination to continue, no matter what the personal cost. Underlying this resolve is the recognition that there is no real choice. It is clear, with the understanding developed so far, that there is no way back.

Pursuing the path with determination, often through times of very considerable discomfort, the meditation begins to change. Moments of equanimity begin to arise and, with them, deep calm, clear observation, far less personal involvement and more mindfulness. The meditator can sit for an hour that goes by so quickly that its ending is a surprise. Even when the meditation stops, the wonderful sense of calm and freshness of vision can persist. It is a delightful state, and a delightful stage of the meditative path.

All of these stages, incidentally, can last for a longer or a shorter time depending upon whether your progress is fast with ease or slow with difficulty, or anything in between. Some people can experience equanimity, for example, over a period of months, sometimes even longer. For some, it comes and goes quite quickly, in an afternoon or a day or two.

The practice leads on to the stage known as 'insight leading to emergence', emergence from the cocoon of the relative world into the clear light of the beyond. One of the three marks—typically transience—is seen everywhere, in everything you examine, in everything you observe, with increasing speed and precision. It is as though the meditator is being swept along. It is altogether different from seeing arising and passing away as it was before, for now the meditator is much more aware of the conditioned nature of the things he sees.

Insight leading to emergence is followed immediately by the first glimpse of the beyond, after which it is impossible to fall back. Getting this far, a meditator has established a permanent foothold on the path and can no longer fall away; he is now certain of coming to enlightenment. This is, therefore, a stage to be aimed at as a minimum achievement, for it removes all worry about the farther future.

Mundane beneficial changes can occur based solely upon self-control, loving-kindness meditation and the general exercise of restraint. For insight to develop, however, there has to be clear comprehension that arises from discrimination and the capacity temporarily to put aside all the hindrances in the seated meditation.

The arising of insight depends upon discrimination and upon access concentration, whereupon the mind is free from hindrances and able to observe clearly; no meditative progress can be made without these two factors. Given these and sufficient application, almost anyone can succeed in the meditation.

What are the benefits of success in insight?

Even before full enlightenment, there is a substantial reduction in craving and hatred, with increasing happiness, as understanding of the cause of suffering becomes more stable. As understanding grows and experience deepens, there arise three knowledges or 'controlling faculties'.

The first knowledge is 'I shall come to know the unknown'. This definite conviction arises quite clearly in the mind. Suddenly, for no immediate reason that you can discern, you become completely confident of eventual success in the practice.

The second is called 'coming to know' and relates to the time and work occurring between the first knowledge and full enlightenment. Here, the meditator is conscious that he is working to 'come to know' the whole truth and still rests content in the knowledge that he will ultimately succeed.

The third knowledge or controlling faculty is 'one who knows'. This knowledge arises with full enlightenment. The being who is free, is enlightened, knows that it is so and knows that his task is complete.

* * *

There are several requirements for successful handling of the burden of meditation. These are not optional: all are necessary if the great prize is to be won. Merely to suffer is not enough.

Although suffering drives the meditative engine—for no one would do any meditative work without being inherently dissatisfied—no progress will be made towards the ultimate cessation of anguish, enlightenment, unless there is at least basic right view or clear comprehension. Basic or mundane right view includes the recognition that ethical actions have results, that there are other planes of existence and that we are reborn according to our deeds. Without the understanding of personal ethical action, and the results of it, no one takes responsibility for or control of his own actions sufficiently to do any useful meditative work, no matter how hard he may try.

Exercising personal restraint by keeping the precepts is not an optional extra, for any successful meditation depends on a mind that is harmonious and free from the agitation and guilt that attend actions that harm others.

Meditation will not succeed without right concentration, at the very least the capacity to overcome the hindrances. Neither self-restraint nor concentration can come to fruition without discrimination or mindfulness and clear comprehension. The fastest progress for any individual is ensured by systematic development of mindfulness, for only mindfulness can show what needs to be done.

Nibbāna is here and now. It is nearer to you than breath itself, nearer than thought, nearer than feeling. All you have to do is open the eye of insight.

12

Suffering, a Gateway to Liberation

or How to Gain Experience of Suffering

A young man I once knew had a wonderfully engaging personality that he used unscrupulously to con people out of money and possessions. Then homeless and looking for a bed for the night, he tried to persuade me that he was sincerely interested in following the Buddha's teaching, hoping that I would let him stay at the Monastery for a few days and give him a little money as well.

I told him that, if he were truly interested in the training, he would have to give up his deception, his thieving and his defrauding of gullible women. His response was interesting and not very different from many who start meditation but find the restraint hard to bear. He maintained that it would be better to continue with his wrong actions because, that way, he would suffer more intensely. Because of this, he would become desperate for the teaching and would then apply himself much more effectively.

A large proportion of our lives is dedicated to avoiding or attempting to overcome distress in any of its forms. If discomfort is not currently an issue, then we are probably trying to enhance our lives in some way, for we seldom rest content with circumstances as they are. Instead of allowing life to unfold as it will, we usually prefer to seek greater enjoyment and fulfilment.

Sometimes, we get jaded by the constant struggle to ease the burden or by our many stimulating activities and long for peace and quiet—at least for a while. Perhaps we turn, as have many before us, to the teaching of the Buddha which, we are told, offers a complete answer to the problem of suffering in all its forms.

This wonderful teaching is comprehensive, accurate, systematic, inviting of inspection, comprehensible by the wise, a 'come and see' training worthy of study in depth. It covers every aspect of life, from how to behave for true personal benefit in the most mundane of affairs to the greatest spiritual and philosophical heights known to or knowable by man and *deva*. Ultimately it leads beyond—beyond the worlds of sensuality, form and formlessness—to *nibbāna*.

Nibbāna is the ultimate eradication of suffering through the destruction of ignorance, craving and hatred, the sources of all the ills of the world. That state of peace beyond the relative world is reached by travelling the Buddha's noble eightfold path, eventually to arrive at the supramundane paths and their fruitions.

The transition from supramundane path to fruition for a stream-winner, or any other noble person, is through one of the three gateways to liberation. These are: the gateway to liberation that is transience (*anicca*), the gateway to liberation that is suffering (*dukkha*), the gateway to liberation that is non-self (*anattā*).

Getting to and going through one of the gateways is a matter of accumulating enough wisdom and experience of the particular mark. It is noticeable, for instance, that the initial progress of those who come to meditation is governed by (among other things) the depth of their understanding of suffering. Much experience of suffering, when pondered over, produces what the Buddha called *amoha*, which we translate as non-confusion or wisdom.

Simply to have suffered is not enough—after all, distress and privation, though commonplace, seldom drive people to intense philosophical enquiry. The existence of suffering has to be closely examined and considered at the profoundest level. Non-confusion or wisdom is not an intellectual quality but knowledge born of mindful experience. One with this quality knows, for example, that the siren-song of sensory indulgence belies its treacherous nature. He or she knows that what seems so attractive on the surface burns like fire when grasped at. There is no doubt and no possibility of such knowledge being lost and he sees life as dangerous and painful. Unsurprisingly, those with this understanding often dedicate themselves to the search for peace and quiet.

So, what is the mark of suffering? How do we gain more experience of it in order to progress towards the complete cessation of all distress whatever? Is it wise to attempt to hasten progress, or would we be better advised simply to let life bring events to us?

When defining suffering, the Buddha gave a comprehensive list of things, activities and events that, most would agree, are undeniably things we would prefer to avoid if that were possible.

He said, 'Birth is suffering, decay is suffering, death is suffering; sorrow, lamentation, pain, grief and despair are suffering; to be separated from the loved is suffering; to be conjoined with the unloved is suffering; in short, the five groups of grasping are suffering.'

The *occurrences* of suffering are without number, but the *mark* of suffering is singular. It is that quality of an object or process that we find unsatisfactory, distasteful, unpleasant, unwelcome, painful or irritating; the object is not as we would wish, given a choice.

If our particular conditioning leads us toward the gateway to liberation that is suffering, we make progress in that direction by accumulating experience of the mark of suffering. There are various options.

Is it enough, do you think, just to live our lives normally, reasoning that some of the things that the Buddha defined as suffering are certain to come our way? After all, none of us can avoid accidents or decay and eventual death, and none of us can avoid occasional contact with things we find unpleasant. Is this enough?

It cannot be. We have all lived countless lives before this one—and in each of those we came up against things we would have preferred to avoid, and died, still in ignorance. Those experiences did not bring us recognisably closer to freedom from suffering; ordinary experiences in this life will not do so, either. No, we need something less moderate, something certain to increase our experience of suffering and at the same time to provide the chance of gaining insight into that fundamental mark of conditioned things.

One certain way to increase our experience of suffering is to follow the *wrong* eightfold path. It has to be said that there is no wisdom in this course but there is unquestionably a dramatic increase in pain and distress.

The wrong eightfold path consists of wrong view, wrong aspiration, wrong action, wrong livelihood, wrong speech, wrong effort, wrong mindfulness and wrong concentration. In all of these, 'wrong' means contrary to fact. For instance, wrong view might include the (false) idea that there is nothing after death; wrong action—murder, theft, exploitation and the like—is wrong because of the false view behind it that personal gratification can be achieved at others' expense and without any damage to oneself. Trying to live at variance with reality causes a kind of friction or resistance for the wrongdoer, increasing his suffering in proportion to the degree of ignorance of the true functioning of the mental and physical universe.

The wrong eightfold path, just like the right one, is divided into three sections: *sīla*, *samādhi* and *paññā*.

Wrong *sīla*, or wrong self-discipline, is essentially behaviour that is selfish and inconsiderate of the welfare of others.

Wrong meditation (comprising wrong effort, wrong mindfulness and wrong concentration) is meditation to enhance self; it is meditation for material or mental gain as opposed to true welfare. The Venerable Chögyam Trungpa rightly called it 'spiritual materialism'.

Wrong views and aspirations are of two types, mundane and supramundane.

Mundane wrong view includes the ideas that actions do not have results, that anything goes as long as you are not found out, that there is no life after death, that there is no particular benefit in being born human (and, therefore, that parents need not be honoured), that there are no other realms of existence, that there are no teachers who can show the way.

Supramundane wrong views—wrong ideas about the path to enlightenment—include the views that things are permanent, satisfactory and independent, that there is a 'core self' that never changes and that ritual attendance at your church or temple of choice is sufficient to guarantee eventual liberation.

All these should be avoided like the plague by those intent on their own well-being. If you wish to follow the true path, then the wrong path is the most dangerous set of views and practices that you could ever find.

The major problem with the wrong path is that, while it does indeed lead to increasing suffering, it also leads to greater levels of confusion, craving and hatred. Unfortunately for the young con-man and all those tempted by continued indulgence, wisdom does not develop further. In fact, it becomes increasingly difficult to make sense of anything and one's chances of recognising an effective way to freedom diminish almost to zero. There has to be a great deal of suffering over a protracted period—some would say over lifetimes—before the faith is born that there must be a better way of living. Only when there is faith, however faint, can there be a search for a way out of the difficulties. Only when the search has been under way, with intelligent investigation, for a long time is it possible to recognise what is, or is not, a worthwhile path to tread.

Another potential problem with indulging until it hurts too much is that it might take so long to work through the sequence of suffering, arousing faith, searching for and finding a path, that the Buddha's teaching could well have died out by the time one would have been ready to follow it.

We do have another option, although some are initially reluctant to commit themselves to it. The best choice is the *right* eightfold path: right view, right aspiration, right action, right livelihood, right speech, right effort, right mindfulness and right concentration. In this setting, 'right' means true to fact as, for instance, in the (right) view that actions do have results. Holding this view, one's actions more closely conform to the laws of the universe and suffering is diminished accordingly. The right path is the mirror image of the wrong one. Where one following the wrong path accentuates selfishness and self-centredness, the student of the right path makes every effort to restrain egocentric behaviour in whatever he does.

I want to look at the right path in some detail for, though following it produces an unquestionable reduction in distress, it is, nevertheless, the finest way to *increase* one's experience of suffering. If that sounds paradoxical, bear with me. All should become clear.

* * *

Practically, the right eightfold path begins with *sīla*, personal discipline or restraint. The factors that make up right discipline are three: right action, right livelihood and right speech.

Right action is action free from the stain of selfishness. In essence, it can be accomplished for the lay person by keeping four of the five precepts (speech, being so difficult, is treated separately), while the recluse has many more rules to keep to ensure his or her action is impeccable. Right action covers all deliberate physical conduct and results in a measure of happiness and freedom from guilt in our relationships, both with other people and with ourselves. It also introduces an element of mindful awareness that is helpful in tackling meditation.

If right action reduces personal distress, not to mention relieving the community of the burden of bad behaviour, how can it increase our awareness of the mark of suffering?

Anyone who has made the effort already knows the answer. Through the attempt to restrain, we become increasingly aware of two things: the selfish nature of our own minds and the intense mental pain we feel when deliberately harming another. What we had previously thought to be a 'buzz' or exciting we see, on closer inspection, to be nothing but anguish. We become much more aware of the mark of suffering, internally and externally, and become rightly fearful of adding to the problem by wrong action.

Right livelihood concerns the way in which we earn the money or goods necessary to live; it is to refrain from occupations that oppress and harm other beings, whether human or animal. The traditional list of proscribed livelihoods includes slavery, trading in weapons or poisons, trading in intoxicants or 'recreational' drugs (yes, they did exist in the Buddha's day), breeding animals for slaughter, killing animals or fish, treachery, fraud, telling fortunes or predicting the future and usury (lending money at extortionate rates of interest).

It is not always easy to avoid harmful occupations. Desperate for a job, one may be tempted to take anything and not look too closely at the consequences. It is not a good idea.

I have heard it said that, as the modern world is 'so much more complicated', we need to add extra wrong means of livelihood to the list. One such suggestion was 'selling goods made by exploited workers'. We need to bear in mind, however, that livelihood, right or wrong, is a question of *kamma*. As such, it is akin to the age-old arguments for and against eating meat. Some maintain, wrongly, that to eat meat is to commit the action of killing. Others realise, as the Buddha himself taught, that buying meat over a counter is a very long way removed from killing an animal with your own hands. As far as *kamma* is concerned, accountability for killing would exist only if five points were fulfilled: there was a being to be killed, there was awareness that it was a being, there was the personal intention to kill that being, there was personal effort made to kill the being, the death of the being resulted from one's own efforts.

Understanding this clearly can save no end of heartache. At the same time, clear comprehension of right livelihood is won only at a cost; looking carefully at the ways in which you might earn a living usually leads to the discovery that someone, somewhere, is being disadvantaged by the things you do. Seldom do you find a job that is wholly beneficial to all involved. Sometimes, to avoid the dilemma of causing distress to others, it seems tempting to choose to avoid working altogether—but then you would either harm yourself through starvation or have to live off others' earnings without offering anything in return.

Wherever we turn, we see the mark of unsatisfactoriness; it cannot be avoided but only ignored temporarily. Truly, the world is a fearful place and there seems nowhere we can find peace. Trying always to do the right thing greatly increases our awareness of the mark of *dukkha*, suffering.

The last of the three factors that make up right discipline is right speech. This is one of the most difficult things to accomplish, especially in the early days when mindfulness is not strong.

There are two areas I think are particularly challenging: humour and gossip.

Humour is often blacker than it at first appears, including as it does facetiousness, mockery or derision. Coming from the root of hatred, such fun at others' expense is initially hard to restrain—but it can be done and the rewards are considerable. Life is unquestionably happier if one is not always 'putting others down'.

Gossip is probably the oldest pastime in the world. Its roots go deep and the pleasure it affords means that it is difficult to see the harm it does. Start paying attention to speech, though, and much is revealed. Gossip, like humour, can be immensely destructive of others' peace of mind and this is reflected in our own states of mind afterwards. Most find that they become aware of a feeling of uneasiness, of dissatisfaction, when their speech has been uncontrolled and harmful to others. There is some embarrassment at having let oneself down, but most pain arises directly from recognition of others' discomfort. Again, awareness of the mark of suffering increases and provides motivation for being ever more scrupulous in following the right eightfold path.

The next major section of the noble eightfold path is right meditation. This consists of right effort, right mindfulness and right concentration.

Right effort is an interesting factor, for so many of us in the West interpret it as maximum effort at all times, no matter what we are trying to accomplish. While a meditator, if caring for someone who is ill, for instance, would not dream of being too forceful, that understanding seems to vanish when applying efforts on his own behalf. Coming to meditation, he gives it everything he has, the quicker to gain the benefits meditation practice has in store for the successful. In consequence, there is a very great increase in distress and pain which makes of the training a battleground of endurance and martyrdom. Others, in complete contrast, indulge themselves in pleasurable feelings and daydreams and do no meditative work at all. There is another way, the *right* way, the middle way.

The traditional four right efforts are:

The effort to overcome hindrances currently arisen
The effort to prevent further hindrances from arising
The effort to bring into existence beneficial states of mind
The effort to maintain beneficial states of mind.

In all cases, the effort is not so much heroic as gentle and *repetitive*. The secret lies not in strength or resignation but in calm and patient persistence, not in brute force or delicate daydream but in calm and patient persistence. But then, our major concern when first coming to the meditation is often to get what we want—whether pleasure or progress—as quickly as possible.

Meditators endeavouring to set up right mindfulness often focus too much on self-achievement. Right mindfulness is unselfconscious, gentle, repetitive and directed towards things that actually exist. For *vipassanā* meditation, the right objects of mindfulness are the fundamental processes of sensory and mental experience. These include things like sight, sound, pressure and touch, heat, feeling, perception, hindrances and states of mind. The content of thinking—the things thought about—are of no consequence as far as meditation is concerned, for it consists of ultimately unreal objects.

To be mindful of 'my progress' or 'Andrea's hairstyle' or of 'redesigning the kitchen' is not sufficient, for these things do not exist in the ultimate sense. Thinking of this kind is personal compilation of many different experiences; it is interpretation, speculation or worry many times removed from the real event that triggered the train of thought. We want to be mindful of the initial stimulus, to see what *really* happens, rather than to play with ideas. So, while ideas are real—in the sense that they exist, as ideas—their content is not an elementary sensory experience. We want to pay attention to the 'building blocks' of experience rather than to the overall building.

Other right objects for right mindfulness are different aspects of materiality and the individual mental concomitants that form the basis of mental states. For instance, mental concomitants include mindfulness, concentration, tranquillity, energy, rapture, ignorance, craving, hatred, faith, intelligence and wisdom. Finally, and most importantly, right objects include the three marks of *anicca*, *dukkha* and *anattā*. All of these exist at the ultimate level and, to that extent, are real.

When, as often happens in the early days, self-view arises, it should be noted, without concern as far as that is possible. Indeed, the secret of success in the meditation is to include every personal reaction. With some training, the first mental conditions that become apparent are things like desire-for-progress, frustration and conceit in the form of comparison with others. These should simply be noted without heat or involvement.

So, how does right mindfulness increase awareness of suffering?

When a meditator first tries to observe mind and body in an unselfconscious way, it is usual for him to find it extremely difficult. The obstacles in the form of the hindrances are all based on self-view in one form or another and consequently the emphasis is on self-gratification. This shows itself either as a desire for comfort and pleasure, with consequent unwillingness to face discomfort, or as a strong desire for results, which leads to tension, difficulty and pain.

In both cases, development of the meditation is impossible until the hindrances have been overcome, at least temporarily, and suffering becomes very apparent. If the practice is dreamy and unfocused, no work is done and the meditator feels guilty. If it is tense and painful, right meditation—viewed as calm and stable attention to the right objects—begins to look like an impossible dream.

The attempt to establish right concentration suffers from similar difficulties. Instead of quiet focus on the meditation object and simple letting go of distractions, there is often a fight with the obstacles to the practice. Instead of attending systematically to the hindrances, the meditator either goes to sleep or tries to blast through the murk into the calmness he is sure must be waiting around the corner.

Developing skill in the practice is very much a question of learning how to put self-concern aside, of learning how to get out of one's own light, as it were. The most common 'method' is that of trial and error—and the errors are often many and painful. There is no question that learning how to practise right concentration can increase one's understanding of suffering—through despair over the intractability of the lazy mind, through pain and agitation from over-effort and also through recognising the pernicious states that commonly arise in the untrained mind.

There is also the fact that success in concentration is something of a two-edged sword. It gives access to deliciously calm and tranquil states of mind—the very thing that those strongly aware of suffering most want—but accentuates by comparison the coarseness and painfulness of the everyday world. To overcome the apparent dilemma we need to look at the third section of the eightfold path, that of wisdom or understanding.

Right understanding consists of two factors, right view and right aim or aspiration. The noble eightfold path was designed to allow those who choose to follow it to eradicate completely every kind of suffering. Wisdom is the culmination of the journey and the last step before full freedom.

If wisdom is so beneficial, how could it actually enhance one's experience of suffering? Would we not expect it to bring tranquillity? Let us see.

Right view is that view which is closest to the real facts of existence. It covers a wide spectrum and usually starts with an intellectual appreciation of, for instance, the fact that actions have results. It grows, still intellectually, into an appreciation that things are transient, unsatisfactory and non-self. At this level right view is really right belief, for the individual does not know for a fact; he or she takes on trust, and as seemingly reasonable, the information provided by another.

At the other end of the spectrum of right view is direct, living experience of the real facts of existence. Here, the individual *sees* the facts and thus knows beyond any possibility of contradiction that they are true. Belief is left behind in favour of experiential knowledge; one knows directly and has no need of belief.

So, what is known for a fact, through experience? It is known for a fact that things are unsatisfactory. The painful and unsatisfactory nature of every conditioned thing has been not only pondered over but also directly experienced. One knows for certain, through experiencing it for oneself, that things are ultimately unsatisfying—that there can be no lasting happiness in the world of the conditioned, however exalted, however humble. Already the mind is beginning to turn away from the relative universe towards the peace of the beyond.

Right aspiration or right aim, sometimes translated as right thought, is to point one's mind in the 'right' direction. In this case, 'right' means in the direction of decreasing suffering, ultimately to eradicate it altogether.

But, even here, there is difficulty: if we constantly aim at a state free from suffering and distress, what are we most aware of? In nearly every case, its opposite: the states associated with anguish and unsatisfactoriness. So right aim, or right thought, also increases our awareness of the mark of conditioned phenomena which is suffering.

Travelling the right eightfold path is *the one way* to the eradication of suffering. But, as many teachers in many situations have advised, it is essential to know your enemy. Enemies preventing the success of the spiritual traveller's search are attachment to suffering itself and the belief that permanent happiness or peace can be found in the world.

Following the path that the Buddha laid down so many centuries ago, a meditator learns about suffering in every area of his life. The mark of suffering is evident throughout, from pain and difficulty when trying to establish right action, livelihood and speech, through self-conscious tensions when setting up right mindfulness and concentration, to the uncomfortable realisations in experiences of right view and right thought. Indeed, without the mark of suffering there would be no path. Remember the direct knowledge of the four noble truths that the Buddha won at enlightenment? The first was, 'There is suffering.'

Not until the meditator knows about every aspect of suffering *from experience* can he approach the narrow gateway to liberation that is suffering.

Through walking the path and constantly refining the meditation, the mind becomes pliable, skilled in observation and free from hindrances. No longer swayed by every passing thought or contact, the meditator experiences deep equanimity—meditations pass with alert tranquillity and with little sense of time; things that once would have provoked intense frustration are now accepted easily and comfortably. There is confidence, skill and clear comprehension of the task.

Concentration is strong and awareness keen. Contemplating the mark of suffering the meditator sees ever more clearly—though without concern—that there can be no peace where it exists. Everywhere he looks, the mark of *dukkha* is present and the knowledge arises, born of experience, that there can be no escape from suffering within the conditioned mind or body. The mind becomes disenchanted with the mental and physical universes and, recognising that the problem is the constant grasping at, the desire for, conditioned things, turns away from all of them to enter the gateway to liberation that is suffering. Passing through, the meditator attains the first fruition, thereby becoming a streamwinner. At that time, the most obvious thing about the fruition experience is the absence of desire or craving—which is why it is known as the 'desireless liberation'.

There is still much to do but, with this supramundane attainment, the meditator joins the ranks of the great ones and final success is certain. He or she has at most seven lifetimes before enlightenment—and that is assuming that no more work is done in this lifetime. However, for those contemplating the mark of suffering, the world is seen as a terrifyingly dangerous place. Consequently, most choose to keep working at the noble eightfold path, the quicker to come to the place of peace where all suffering ceases forever and there is no more to do.

The Buddha's path, with its complete set of instructions on how to come to the ending of all distress, is still available and effective today. It can still be travelled successfully by those who dare to challenge their own preconceived ideas and theories with real, meditative experience. The way is not easy—indeed, it will cost you everything you depend on psychologically—but it is the most worthwhile venture you can imagine. Tasting the nectar of the beyond, one is forever drunk with freedom and no more a victim of the ills of the world.

13

Emptiness

To find the highest happiness, the Buddha said, you have first to know how this life works; it is no use speculating about a possible future rebirth or regretting the past. It is what we do now that is important. Indeed, the only place and time we can do anything to free ourselves from our chains is here and now; we can act in no other time or place.

It is perhaps a truism that every being values its own life. Self-preservation is one of the strongest instincts and few, human or non-human, would choose to die, given the option.

But stronger even than love of life for human beings is love of self. Many would defend their principles, their self-view, their 'rights', even at the cost of their own lives. Most of us view life from a perspective that can only be called self-centred. It is no exaggeration to say that dearest to every human being is his or her self.

The one aspect of Buddha-Dhamma that causes intense concern to those who value individuality and self-development is the Buddha's teaching on non-self. Often poorly understood, non-self is almost certain to raise doubts in those new to the teaching. Even some university-level material in this country, in England, wrongly suggests that the aim of the Buddhist teaching is 'extinction of the personality'.

So, what is the goal of Buddha-Dhamma? Is it annihilation of the self, as some claim? Is the end-point of the training a black and featureless emptiness, where nothing exists?

The goal of Buddha-Dhamma is nothing less than the eradication of all suffering. This is attained through the generation of insight wisdom that eradicates craving and confusion based on wrong views of the world. Specifically, insight wisdom overcomes the three 'hallucinations of perception' that things are permanent, capable of producing lasting happiness, and self or belonging to self.

The Buddha taught that all things are transient, unsatisfactory and without a self. What did he mean by that? He meant that all things are transient, unsatisfactory and without a self—literally.

We usually know that the things we speak of as 'permanent' are only relatively long-lasting. If we accept the Buddha's maxim, 'Any change in a thing is a change of thing,' it is easy to see, intellectually, that nothing lasts for very long at all. Every change of state means that a thing is no longer the same: it is now a different entity, with different qualities. It is not so much that things change but that they 'die', to be replaced by something new. Things are transient.

Unquestionably there is happiness in the world—which would seem to contradict the Buddha's statement that all things are unsatisfactory—but happiness cannot be made to last, cannot be relied upon, and is built upon very shaky foundations. The things that produce happiness are themselves transient and, to that extent, unsatisfactory. Most of us can accept this, also. From this point of view, things are unsatisfactory.

As for self, that seems to be a more difficult problem. We all, when untrained, feel that we have a self.

If this self does exist, then we have to be able to perceive it, the things it owns and the qualities it has. If the self is permanent, then it can of course never change (for any change in a thing is a change of thing). If the self can never change, then no quality of the self can ever change, for exactly the same reason. So the self must always exhibit the same perceivable qualities; it must be in the same state permanently.

But perhaps it is the things that the self possesses that change, while the self stays the same, permanently? If so, the self must at different times be possessed of different things—and therefore must itself be different to that extent, so that cannot be the answer.

Perhaps the self can never be known, its attributes not being perceivable? If this is so, and we could never know the self, then we are playing imagination games and could dream up anything we like to be the self, for we could never find out whether we were right or not.

All this would seem to work in theory, as it were, but how can we prove conclusively that the unchanging self either does or does not exist? There is only one way: we have to examine the details of our inner and outer experience in which we will find—if it should exist—the self we believe we have.

The problem we face immediately is the very thing we need to overcome—lack of awareness, ignorance, of the way in which mind and body work.

We need to distinguish, by direct experience, the different components and processes of mind and body. The Buddha's teaching gives us a way to do exactly that through the setting up of mindfulness. With practice, we become able to perceive mental and physical processes that were previously invisible to us.

Above all else, we need a clear idea of what is real and what is not. We would all agree, I am sure, that the things we dream about at night are very often so fantastic, so unlikely and so unreal that we have no hesitation in putting them down to imagination. We do not believe they are real in any significant way.

What can we identify as unquestionably real? It is more difficult than it at first appears. Is a car 'real'? The initial reaction is that it is— and they are getting to be a real problem, these days, with grid-lock in every large town and city. But are we correct in assuming a car is a real object? We have to say that in one way it is and in another way it is not.

Relatively speaking, a car does of course exist but, when examined closely, and bearing in mind that 'any change in a thing is a change of thing', we can see that the car is not the same for any two consecutive moments. If it never changed, it would never wear out, get dirty nor use petrol or oil. A car is not an ultimately real thing. It is an assemblage of components all of which change and decay. Something that is ultimately real cannot be divided into smaller parts; it is not a compound structure of other identifiable pieces or processes.

We can apply the same reasoning to human experience. The human being is an assemblage of parts—a body and a mind, at the simplest level. These cannot be ultimately real because they subdivide into smaller, discrete elements of experience.

'Body', by which we mean all materiality whatever, traditionally consists of 'earth, air, fire and water', these being its ultimate constituents from the point of view of experience, and twenty-four material qualities derived from these.

Earth is hardness or softness to the sense of touch, and shape or colour to the sense of sight. Air is motion. Fire is heat, either warm or cold. Water is the cohesive force that keeps the other three great elements together. Any experience of matter can be proven through personal experience to consist of these ultimately real things.

The twenty-four derived material qualities include the sense organs and sense objects, expression through gesture, expression through speech, and the like. These, taken together, describe every possible experience of materiality, whether past, present or future.

'Mind' is more complex and is divided into four collections of similar kinds of experiences—feelings, perceptions, mental components of behaviour and consciousness.

There are only five feelings: bodily pleasant, bodily unpleasant, mentally pleasant, mentally unpleasant, mentally neutral.

The perceptions number six: visible form, sound, odour, taste, bodily impression, mental impression.

There are fifty components of behaviour, usually referred to as the group of mental formations or, sometimes, volitional tendencies. They include not only craving, hatred, ignorance, but also contact, volition, attention, pride, fear of blame, pliancy of mind, pliancy of mental properties, joy, happiness, depression and many others.

Consciousness is treated in several different ways, depending on the level of analysis. At its simplest, this collection comprises six elements: consciousness by way of eye, ear, nose, tongue, body and mind.

Analysed by states of consciousness as opposed to sensory data, the group consists of eighty-nine different states. For example, there is 'Consciousness accompanied by pleasure, associated with knowledge, prompted'. Or, 'Consciousness accompanied by displeasure, associated with hatred, unprompted'. Included in the group are supramundane states such as 'Path consciousness of stream-entry' and 'Fruition consciousness of arahantship'.

Buddha-Dhamma provides an exhaustive analysis of all levels of experience. It includes what most consider 'normal'; it includes meditative states and everything else besides. There exist beyond the sensory universe two other distinct levels—the world of form and the formless world. In the former, all experience through the five bodily senses is left behind so that the individual lives for the time being in a world made up of fine material substance, or form. In the formless world, even this fine materiality is left behind and experience is of pure consciousness.

It is not theory. The analysis is objective, being derived from meditative observation of both gross and subtle levels of personal experience, and experience of these states is repeatable, given adequate training.

Why analyse so exhaustively? The Buddha discovered that suffering arises because of craving based on ignorance that the things we choose to depend on in life are unreliable in every way and cannot bring us the happiness we all seek. In other words, our view of the world—including our view of self—is inaccurate and causes us to suffer.

Unaware of the perils, we commit blunder after blunder by relying on certain things and activities to bring us satisfaction when they are incapable of doing so.

Sensual pleasures are a favourite pastime and account for much of the world's wealth, since people are willing to pay dearly for their indulgences. But, as any serious hedonist will tell you, sensual pleasures pall in excess. More indulgence, far from bringing more and greater pleasure, on the contrary brings increasing dullness and boredom. To get the same 'hit' most are tempted to try something stronger until, if we become 'hooked', there is in the end the distinct danger of depravity and personal ruin. Sensual pleasures are the cause of much strife, even warfare, as greed for this or that prompts men and women to steal their neighbours' land, property, wealth, possessions and partners—or to right 'wrongs' and slights, imagined or real.

Alternatively, we depend on development, on growth and expansion. In this case, we feel cheated if we are not 'fulfilling our potential' or 'bettering ourselves' and spend obsessive amounts of time working to achieve our goals. Those in this category are prepared to put off the pleasures of the moment for the longer-term advantage of money, position, power or knowledge. Not for them a pub-crawl with friends; they would rather attend evening classes or Open University, or meditate. They want to keep on growing, developing, increasing their chosen skills and interests. It makes them feel good but it does of course carry a price: they can never be truly content with what they are and always look for satisfaction in the future, never here and now.

There again, some of us are quite satisfied with things the way they are and do not want them to change. Those in this group are the Luddites of the world, the conservatives and conservationists in every walk of life. Scratch the office-worker who resists the introduction of new procedures and you find under the skin a Luddite who, given the appropriate incentive, will sabotage the new regime by subtle non-compliance and deliberate misunderstanding. Those of us with this outlook view 'progress' with profound suspicion and are often deeply resentful of the erosions of valuable freedoms and traditions that seem inevitably to accompany life today.

Underlying these different dependencies are different views of the world. A view can never be wholly accurate for, like a coin, every issue has two sides, but we tend to believe that our view is a fact, by which we mean a reality. Did you know that the derivation of the word 'fact' is from the Latin *facere*, to make, or *factum*, made thing (as in manu*facture*)? 'Fashion' also comes from the same root, so a fact is something made or fashioned—much as we think of 'fiction' today. Facts are not ultimate reality—scientific 'fact' has changed and changed again over the decades.

Some of us rely on ignoring the things we find unpleasant. We do so by either forming, and clinging to, views about them—which means we don't have to think—or through activities that prevent us noticing what is going on through dulling perception—drink, drugs, excessive work, depression, romance, obsession and indulging in fantasy. In fact, just about anything can serve as an escape if we put our minds to it.

The Buddha's system of analysis, when developed, brings our views and behaviour into line with the ultimate realities of existence. To develop it, we have to examine, with scrupulous attention, the very things we rely on. There is no escaping the task of meditation if we truly wish to prove whether there is or is not a permanent self, or if we wish to conquer distress.

When we start meditation, we tend to view things from a self-centred perspective and place the self—me—at the centre of things. Any gains we expect to accrue to me, my*self*. Any easing of distress we likewise expect to be experienced by me, my*self*. If it is knowledge we seek, again we expect that knowledge to be acquired by me, my*self*. Instructed that all things are not self, we feel distinctly uncomfortable, but still think that the practice will be of benefit—to me, my*self*.

We pay attention to the sensation of rising and falling in the abdomen, and take note of everything else that comes before the eye of attention. We notice sensation in other parts of the body, pleasant and unpleasant feelings, sensory impacts and, of course, thinking. We are identifying the real things in our experience—thinking, smelling, touching, feeling and so on. All these actually exist.

From the meditative point of view, we are not interested in the contents of our fantasies, or in hallucinations. We want to find out what *really* is going on. For instance, discursive thinking certainly exists; there is no question about it. The things thought about, however, are usually a very different story; the contents of thoughts are a chaotic jumble of all kinds of half-formed ideas, fantasies and daydreams. Even when the thinking is more serious, much of it is fantasy and speculation concerning the *me* that I cannot at present prove to exist.

With repeated practice, one thing becomes plain—in any experience, there are only two components: the object that arises and the mind that comprehends it. Every experience follows the same pattern. In this, we can find no self; the process goes on without the need for a controller of any description. Not only that, but it is evident that every experience, past, present and future, must be of the same nature and could not possibly be different. This realisation, though based on experience, is at this stage still largely intellectual and is therefore called 'inferential knowledge of non-self'.

To talk about non-self is perhaps a little premature, for most people have difficulty getting the meditation stable enough to get this far quickly, though some do. Most of us initially find difficulties with the meditation that, at times, seem insuperable. The problems that meditators have in gaining a calm and stable mind are classified as the five hindrances to meditation: sensual desire, ill will, sloth and torpor, worry and flurry and sceptical doubt. It is sometimes helpful to look at these five in a different way. Rather than looking at the obstacles directly, it can help to examine the things that many of us habitually rely on for relaxation or security. The three most significant things in this respect are sensual pleasure, progress and resisting change.

Those of us whose main interest in life is sensual pleasure are typically not concerned about the long-term future, being content to live just for today. As long as we are comfortable, stimulated and enjoying sensual delights, the world seems a good place.

But what happens when disaster strikes and we are made redundant, or suffer ill-health or the breakdown of a relationship? Some of us try meditation as a way to come to terms with the distress. Inevitably, we expect the meditation to provide us with sensual pleasure; we look constantly for sensual pleasure in the practice and adjust our meditative efforts to maximise the pleasure we get.

This proves to be a serious hindrance for, while it is certainly possible to experience sensual pleasure while meditating, to be so attached to it is an obstacle that prevents any clear discrimination. For non-self to be seen, even at the level of inferential knowledge, there needs to be much restraint. The watchwords here are restraint, stoicism, sacrifice and asceticism. With these, everything changes and the meditation develops quickly.

Many of us are not particularly concerned with sensual pleasures but are instead keen to get somewhere in life. Here, we see the hard worker, the dedicated enthusiast, the person who misses meals in the pursuit of his work, hobby or interest. People in this group tend to be 'self-made', working many hours a day to set up businesses or pursue vital interests. For them to feel at ease, they have to be stretched, often to the limit.

When they come to meditation, members of this group place their emphasis on hard work, effort and, above all, progress. Their mental chatter is constant comparison of whether this approach is better than that, whether the meditation is working properly or whether it needs alteration or adjustment. The net result, as many of you know, can be excruciating tension that seems insurmountable.

If they keep going, they usually do learn the lesson always to make haste slowly: the fastest way forward is to be endlessly patient. The watchwords here are relaxation and patience.

The Buddha spoke of those who 'feared states of calm'. You might think it strange that anyone coming to meditation should be uncomfortable about becoming calm in body and mind, but it does happen. Meditators complain that they are losing their grip on the meditation, or describe fear arising 'out of nothing'. Typically, after many hours' paying attention to the rise and fall and fighting the hindrances, the meditation becomes still, quiet and spacious. The internal dialogue stops and there seems at first to be little or nothing going on. Instead of enjoying the peace and tranquillity, those who fear states of calm have a quite different response. When peace steals into the mind, they panic.

Sundered from the familiar noise and chatter, divorced from the comfortable familiarity of fantasy, comparisons and external sensations, the meditator is marooned in a sea of apparent nothingness with no guiding marks and nothing to get hold of. When this occurs, most initially beat a hasty retreat to the familiar mental chatter and struggle. It can take many repetitions, and a lot more work, before the fear subsides. Some of us are at first very reluctant to venture outside known space.

Conditioning leads us to seek sensual pleasure, progress or the stasis of the familiar. Each of these is an obstacle to the meditation and has to be addressed if understanding is to grow. The solution to the difficulties they cause in the meditation lies in discrimination of the ultimates of experience, plus some not-so-common common-sense.

In every case, the first step in overcoming a difficulty is to acknowledge what is going on. No matter what your personal problem, to pursue the quest successfully you have to see and acknowledge aspects of experience both loved and hated. In doing so, it is important to see what is real and to deal only with those things. For instance, worry is real but the things worried about are not. Sensual desire is real, but the things imagined are not, except as mental pictures. We need firstly to identify the components of experience and then to examine them. We then can discount those that are unreal, like fantasies, and examine more closely those that are real, like feelings, say, or mental objects.

While you may fervently wish otherwise, you can only start from where you are. If you are tense, worried and uncertain, then these are the things that you should acknowledge. A word of warning: to acknowledge something does not mean to indulge it, to play with it as the tongue seems always to probe a sore tooth. To acknowledge something is to admit its existence, recognise that it is transient—and to move on.

Having learned to see things previously ignored, the meditator can now examine each one. If it disappears from attention, it is, by that fact alone, transient. A transient phenomenon cannot be a foundation for lasting happiness, so it is also unsatisfactory, no matter how pleasant, or unpleasant, for that matter. Lastly, it cannot be the permanent, unchanging self the meditator believes he has.

Sometimes, there are difficulties. A meditator faced with persistent pain may begin to despair. Or perhaps someone develops a sense of futility and falls into doom and gloom about the state of the world and the state of his own life. There is always a solution, though.

One of the finest remedies for self-pity or undue preoccupation with personal distress is to remind yourself, 'This is not me, this is not mine, this is not the self of me.' These most unsatisfactory, hurtful and unpleasant things cannot be the self of me which, if it were to exist, would be permanently enjoyable.

As the meditation unfolds, it becomes increasingly obvious how interlinked things are. If there is a noise, a functional ear and attention, hearing takes place—it cannot be otherwise. I, as a nominal 'self', have no say in the matter at all; the hearing process is conditioned and non-self.

As the Buddha said, 'This arising, that arises; this ceasing, that ceases.'

With more experience, we see that all of the senses operate in the same way. If there is a stimulus, a functioning sense-base and attention, there is inevitably a response and there is nothing we can do about it. It is all non-self; it operates without my permission, it does it by itself. Truly, we are redundant in the most fundamental way.

The same is true of mental experience: given a stimulus arising through a physical sense or from the mind itself—an unbidden memory, say—there is unavoidably a mental response. There is nothing we can do about it; it occurs without our permission; we cannot escape it nor stop it. Indeed, it has already happened by the time that we become aware of it. Mental responses, too, of whatever kind, are non-self; they are not the self of me.

However deeply concentrated or mindful we become, we find the same to be true. The ultimate constituents of everything within the sphere of mental and physical experience, including both the form and formless worlds, are transient, unsatisfactory and non-self. Not only that, but the interaction between the ultimates of experience is free from any trace of a self. It all goes on quite happily and efficiently without anyone taking charge of it or managing it in any way. The so-called self turns out to be the biggest confidence trick in the universe. It does not exist, it never did exist and it certainly will not exist in the future.

Any talk of 'annihilating the self' is so much hot air. There is not and never has been a self to annihilate. All we can get rid of is our wrong idea about self. It is our view of self that is wrong, nothing else.

No matter how we take it apart, no matter how we put it together, the human being—in its entirety or as a collection of parts and processes—is everywhere and always non-self.

Realising non-self is not the final task. In the end, we have to go altogether beyond form and formless, beyond self and non-self. Until that time, though, it helps to remember the following verse, often quoted as a shorthand description of the Buddha's path:

'There is suffering, but no one who suffers.
'Doing exists though there is no doer.
'Extinction exists but no extinguished self.
'Though there is a path, there is no traveller.'

The world is empty of self. The path is empty of self. Enlightenment is empty of self. We can never fall into emptiness, for we are there already.

14

Progress on the Path

There are five factors necessary to make progress on the path to enlightenment. They are an abiding desire to find truth, freedom from external hindrances, freedom from internal hindrances, insight wisdom and a reliable source of guidance. For successful practice, a meditator must have all of these, although the degree of each will naturally vary from person to person.

Some will become enlightened in this lifetime, no matter what obstacles they meet, because their desire to find the truth drives them to develop the other four factors. Some will be unable to complete the path in this lifetime no matter how hard they work and no matter how ideal their circumstances.

The major difference between these two kinds of people is the depth of life experience they have accumulated. This, in essence, means that the difference lies in their understanding of *dukkha*, the unsatisfactory nature of mundane existence, whether that mundane existence is material, mental or abstract.

Of course, most people fall between the extremes. They can become enlightened in this lifetime, but they need help to do so. That is what the Dhamma is for. That is what the Order is for. That is why the Buddha taught as he did.

There are several levels of assistance available to those more or less intent on the spiritual search, though their effectiveness in reducing suffering varies greatly.

Books are a great source of information and may provide the spur to effective, personal action. Without acting on information gleaned in this way, however, books are next to useless and reading becomes simple entertainment or study for its own sake.

Potentially more useful is peripheral contact with an effective way to truth. This would include going to an occasional meeting, rather like going to church on Sundays, without any personal application to the teaching. It helps a little, as it improves one's acquaintance with the teaching and may provide the incentive to seek instruction.

Much more useful is meditating as a lay person. Strong commitment to a teaching centre, with sincere efforts to practise meditation and to study the Buddha's teaching, can be fulfilling in every respect.

By far the most rewarding way of undertaking the meditative path is full-time training. Live-in training provides twenty-four hour a day contact with the teaching in what is probably the most supportive environment possible to find. Embarking on such a course is to cut loose from the commitments of family and friends and to devote one hundred percent of your time to the study and practice of the Dhamma. Without question, full-time training gives the very best chance of mental development, and of eventual enlightenment in this lifetime. It provides the finest environment for the practice of the Dhamma.

Another important factor is to train with a competent teacher. The overwhelming majority of those seeking truth and freedom definitely need experienced and knowledgeable guidance.

The Buddha described his Dhamma, his teaching, as *ehi passiko*, 'come and see'. When speaking in a town one day, he was asked by the inhabitants how, from those professing to teach a spiritual way, they could tell who taught the genuine article and who did not. The Buddha said categorically that no one should believe anything just because somebody said so. Everything should be tested, so that when one knew *from one's own experience* that something was good or bad, then he or she could assess the worth of the particular teacher. Of course, to find out from one's own experience if instruction is worthwhile means that it has to be followed faithfully for long enough to develop the skills to gain the experience—something that many of us in the West have little patience with.

So, how do you improve your own chances of progressing on the spiritual path?

It depends to an extent on the kind of person you are. Classifying people into types is a risky occupation, for it tends to overlook the fact that people can change, and change quite markedly, given the right sort of effort. Even if you suspect that you may be one of the two extreme types mentioned earlier, those who will progress in any event and those who will not, it would be wise to be cautious unless you are *certain* of your judgement.

People can and do change. As far as the meditation goes, I have seen individuals undergo radical changes I would previously not have thought possible. The changes came about dependent on a marked increase in life experience and a consequent increase in determination.

* * *

How can you deliberately set out to improve your chances? We come back to the factors essential for progress. Let us look at each in turn.

First, desire to find the truth. We have to increase our level of urgency. This is a matter of developing more insight into *dukkha*, the fundamentally unsatisfactory nature of the mundane world. The more clearly we perceive *dukkha*, the more we will wish to seek the beyond.

There are various things that prompt personal enquiry in this way. One of the more obvious is bereavement. The sudden loss of someone close will often drive people to question their lives and their reasons for living. The grief, the suffering, drives them to look more deeply than they have done before. The same is true of divorce. A separation or a divorce is harrowing no matter how well-mannered it might be, and may give rise to thoughts about the meaning of life. Terminal illness can provide similar impetus to search into the true nature of things. Major life-changes often accentuate *dukkha*, unsatisfactoriness, sometimes to an unbearable degree.

Natural disaster can provide a similar spur to enquiry. The news this evening carried a story about a volcanic eruption in the Philippines. The suffering is great. People are dying. Lava is swallowing houses and fields, destroying homes and livelihoods as it advances. Those caught up in such terrible disasters are often prompted to enquire deeply into what life is all about. What are the most important things? What should we take as our priorities? Where can our efforts do the most good?

Deep and determined enquiry into questions like these can lead to greater understanding of, and acquaintance with, the unsatisfactory nature of the world. Personal tragedy of any kind places a strain on our easy acceptance of 'normal life'. All disasters induce questions and promote reflection on the unsatisfactory nature of human existence. A strong desire to find the truth is a principal element conditioning success in the spiritual search.

* * *

The second factor essential to progress is freedom from external hindrances. External hindrances are circumstances or activities that block any real chance of progress. They have to be at the very least minimised drastically if you are to progress. This may involve re-ordering your life goals, which you will do only if you perceive more clearly the unsatisfactory nature of things.

The external hindrances are many. If you are constantly worried about your financial situation, you cannot settle to meditate. The same is true about relationship problems. If your relationship starts to go sour, then you may find meditation impossible for the time being.

Another external hindrance is having extreme family commit-ments. If you look after a chronically sick relative or child, there may be little opportunity for anything else. The same is true for parents having to look after a new baby. This kind of caring is extremely time-consuming, leaving little time or energy to pursue the medita-tive goal.

Other kinds of circumstances that hinder the meditation—but over which we have more control—include excessive socialising or working to excess. While many see nothing wrong in a full social calendar it is, without doubt, a great hindrance to the meditative life. A high-pressure job, where your reputation or job-security is constantly on the line, is also a problem in this regard. You may have to work long hours every day just to keep your job safe. Perhaps there is so much work that you can rarely clear the backlog before the next day begins. These situations are unpleasant, to say the least, and completely sap your energies and reduce enthusiasm for meditation.

External hindrances are a definite problem. Take stressful employ-ment, for example. When attempting to meditate, the mind is unavoidably filled with thoughts and worries about the job, the quota or the deadline. It might take you fifteen, twenty or even thirty minutes to put that aside, if you manage to drop it at all. If you did not have the stress in the first place, you would not lose that time and would, therefore, stand more chance of progressing with the practice.

The external hindrances produce on-going agitation in the form of worry or intense attachment. No matter how 'chilled-out' the individual, there are severe stresses inherent in the very circumstances of excessive busyness, however brought about. While external hindrances are present, it is not possible to avoid the kind of stress that prevents effective application to a meditative way. Referring to exactly this kind of thing, the Buddha said, 'Dusty is the household life.' The dust gets in your eyes to the point where you cannot see, and have no hope of developing the eye of insight while those conditions last.

The most effective means of overcoming these difficulties is to become a monk or a nun. Such a step wipes out many of these obstacles at a stroke. The monk is one who, 'Putting aside his circle of relations, shaving hair and beard, donning the robe ... goes forth into the homeless life'. There is no finer way of travelling the meditative path, for the conditions under which recluses live are usually designed to be as supportive as possible. It seems an extreme step to some but, while enlightenment can certainly be attained in lay life, it is very much more difficult and demands a level of restraint few can manage without severe disruption to their lifestyle. Of course, as the Japanese saying has it, there is many a shaven head with a hairy mind; the purpose of removing yourself from external obstacles is negated if, as a monk, you remain continually preoccupied with them.

* * *

The third of the factors essential to making progress on the path is freedom from internal hindrances including, of course, freedom from preoccupation with worldly matters. The traditional list of five hindrances includes sensual desire, ill will, sloth and torpor, flurry and worry, and sceptical doubt. It is unquestionably the case that these prevent progress. They have to be overcome, at the very least during the seated practice some of the time. So intransigent can they be that, sometimes, ancillary meditations such as loving-kindness or the recollections—discursive thinking on specially chosen uplifting subjects—may be needed to bring them under control and to quieten the mind.

It is not uncommon for meditators to be frightened of pleasant states of mind. Familiar with inefficient states, attached to them, they feel cast adrift when they start to disappear. As harbingers of calm arise in the mind, many meditators become anxious that they will lose something vital, that they will be diminished by the loss, however temporary, of a hindering state of mind. The uncertainty promoted by this fear has to be overcome before the meditation can proceed successfully.

Let us look at each of the major hindrances to see how this works.

When trying to restrain sensual desire some, fearing the loss of pleasure, focus only on what they appear to be giving up and sensual and sexual indulgences become a mental preoccupation. When trying to describe the problem, these individuals claim that they have no control over the process, saying that it seems as if the mind is invaded by the persistent and often worrying thoughts and images. Often, they grasp at the worry about the meditation, and this further concern over sensuality and indulgence also helps to sabotage any attempts to attain calm and concentrated states.

The apparent dilemma is often due to confusion between sensual craving and sensory experience. The suppression of sensual craving does not destroy sensory experience. If there are functioning sense organs and appropriate objects in range, pleasant and unpleasant sensory contacts must arise; there is, therefore, no basis for the fear of loss. It is not the sensory objects that are the problem but rather the craving for them. The absence of sensual desire is blissful and much more enjoyable than the dissatisfaction inherent in always wanting more or different stimuli.

In spite of the pain that hindrances cause, people are attached to them and are afraid to let them go. This applies not only to sensual desire but also to ill will, sloth and torpor, worry and flurry, and sceptical doubt.

Those with a tendency to cling to ill will feel very uncomfortable with the unfamiliar peacefulness that prevails in its absence. On a residential course, a student with a strong hate root was instructed to practise loving-kindness meditation for the entire week. It worked. It worked very well. Much to her surprise, she revelled in the loving-kindness, taking to it with facility and enthusiasm. On the last day, however, she experienced an intense reaction against the bliss she had been experiencing. She felt that she had been untrue to herself, that she had been acting out-of-character. Although she had undeniably uncovered a wellspring of loving-kindness within, it was at odds with her picture of herself as a mean and nasty individual. Shaken—and preferring her old view-of-self—she rejected loving-kindness and, as far as I know, continues to reject it to this day. She prefers, instead, to be bitter, angry and full of hatred. Even knowing that she is capable of love, bliss and lightness of mind, she nevertheless prefers the darkness. Fear of pleasant states can be difficult to overcome, especially if someone clings strongly to self-view.

The third internal hindrance is sloth and torpor. This manifests as a lazy, sludgy state of mind, often close to sleep. There may be some daydreaming with an occasional dim awareness of the meditative task in hand. It is warm and comfortable for the most part, although there is often dissatisfaction about not being able to direct the mind, which appears heavy and intractable. Here, too, individuals cling, in this case to a state of warm confusion. It is at least not physically painful. It does not involve any hard work. It is even possible to have a quiet doze and to finish the 'meditation' feeling refreshed, though, of course, none the wiser.

When this hindrance is overcome, the darkness and intractability of mind completely disappear. The mental universe is light, bright, easy to work with and a joy to observe. But some people view clarity and mental finesse with distrust, fearing that they will 'take away the magic'. Afraid of the lightness and brightness, they prefer to cling to the murk and the warmth, which at least have the bonus of allowing dreams full rein.

Agitation or flurry and worry are a problem for those who are excessively forceful or anxious. These produce physical and mental tension with corresponding agitation of mind. Forcefulness leads to mental running here and there, never staying still. Anxiety leads to obsessive concern with the future to the extent that, even if there is apparently nothing to worry about, the meditator will find something, anything, to indulge the habit.

The trouble is that excessive force in the meditation can produce some of the marks of concentration—notably bright lights (*nimitta*)—albeit only for an instant. Such results may look promising to the beginner, but the forcefulness also produces such violent agitation that there is no conceivable way that the concentrated state could ever be sustained.

It can be helpful to see the mind as a series of strata, with agitated and superficial states at the top, dream and sleep at the bottom, and balanced, alert, calm states in the middle. Using this model, the use of excessive force is a little like mental 'bungey-jumping'. It forces the attention down through the layers of mind, briefly touching them all, but because of the nature of force the attention bounces straight back up again, into agitation and flurry. Using this apparent 'shortcut' is counter-productive and it is impossible for the mind to stay in the middle, balanced layers so desired by the meditator.

Forcefulness in the meditation can be difficult to relinquish, not least because our culture praises hard work and self-sacrifice. One would-be meditator refused for ten years to accept that forcefulness was the problem he had to overcome. In all that time he never managed to restrain his urge to force the mind onto the meditation object and would not listen to instruction. Why? Because, whenever he tried to moderate his efforts, he became afraid. The fear took several forms: fear of blame (for not trying hard enough), fear of failure, fear of ease, fear of relinquishing control, fear of tranquillity and so on. In short, he was afraid of the calm, tranquil states that come from the correct use of energy.

Worry is a slightly different case, though the results are somewhat similar. Obsessively concerned with, say, progress, the meditator constantly worries about whether or not he is doing the meditation correctly. So much time is spent in this concern that little actual meditation ever gets done. Again, the anxiety arises from the belief that the meditation cannot work properly without a full and 'proper' (i.e. excessive) investigation of what is going on. Suggest to such a meditator that he relax, take it easy and enjoy the meditation and he will look at you as if you are teaching heresy. There is a definite fear of the pleasant states that arise in the absence of worry.

The last of the five traditional hindrances is sceptical doubt. This is to be distinguished from worry. Worry is concerned to find the best way to implement the teaching through the meditation; it has no doubt that the way itself is valid. The meditator practising sceptical doubt, on the other hand, calls into question the very accuracy or, sometimes, suitability, of the Buddha's teaching. Sceptical doubt often arises from the attempt to compare another religious way with the current one, not realising that the very bases of comparison are flawed. Sometimes it arises from having trouble with the meditation or finding that a particular instruction from the meditation teacher triggers mental resistance. When sceptical doubt is in the ascendant, there is a ready criticism for any- and everything connected with the meditative path and those who walk it, and the hindrance of ill will is often not far away.

Many of those who indulge this hindrance find they cannot let go of criticism and doubt, believing that these things mark them as rational intellectuals. From the meditative standpoint, sceptical doubt is the hallmark of lack of faith on the one hand and lack of experience on the other. Intellectuality—or doubt—can never uncover the mystery of practical meditation; experience is the bedrock of wisdom.

Those who exercise sceptical doubt are often afraid of the comfortable certainty of faith or confidence, which they equate with dullness. Fearful of being gullible, they question, analyse and pull apart the teaching, which, when there is no attempt to learn from the reality of experience, can only be destructive. Analysis is important, but it needs to be done in the right way.

The five mental actions of sensual desire, ill will, sloth and torpor, worry and flurry, and sceptical doubt are called hindrances for a very good reason: they hinder or obstruct the meditation by setting up internal discord. They occupy the mind with irrelevancies and quite prevent the quietness and precision needed for true seeing to take place. The hindrances must be suppressed, at least some of the time, for the meditation to progress.

* * *

We come now to the fourth factor needed for progress on the path. So far, we have dealt with desire to find the truth, freedom from external hindrances and freedom from internal hindrances. Also needed for progress is insight, *vipassanā*.

Those new to meditation often classify their practice as good or bad depending on the degree of comfort they experience: a 'good' meditation is easeful, a 'bad' one, painful. There is much more to it than that.

Overcoming hindrances is but a step on the way, not an end in itself. A truer measure would be the amount of insight generated in any one session. Penetrative insight into transience is the key to progress towards enlightenment, along with insight into *dukkha* (suffering) and *anattā* (non-self). Insight into *anicca*, *dukkha* and *anattā* are three gateways to total freedom from ignorance.

With freedom from hindrances, there is generally freedom from bodily discomfort. With the distractions arising from tension and excessive effort temporarily banished, with harmful states of mind put to one side for the time being, we have the ideal conditions for the development of insight.

Insight into transience can be developed from humble beginnings. Consider, for example, the world on which we live. At some point in the far future, so scientists tell us, the sun will explode, the earth will be burned to a cinder and all life on this planet will cease. While transience on this aeonic time-scale may seem irrelevant, it does help the meditator to realise that even our planet will not be around forever.

We could also consider the social order. It appears to be stable, at least here in the West, and yet we have only to look through historical records to realise that it certainly is not. There are those who propose that we should keep the English race 'pure', that we should not let it change. Our very history is one of change, of the old being replaced by the new. Britain has been invaded and occupied many times in the last few thousand years, and many would argue that our very strength derives from the complex mix of nationalities that has resulted from invasion and empire.

Social orders change, and change very rapidly too. If we seek comfort from the stability of the social order, a quick look at history should prove that our confidence would be misplaced.

The once famed British Empire does not exist any more. Looking at maps of the world going back a hundred years, we can clearly see the extent of the vast Empire 'on which the sun never set'. Much of the land area was coloured pink, representing dominion over millions upon millions of people. The Empire did not last. Empires, like everything else, are transient.

Some individuals yearn to live forever in their current physical body. Someone with this problem may have his corpse frozen with instructions to thaw it only when medical science has 'advanced' sufficiently to cure all his ills and restore him to youthful good health.

As far as physical bodies go, there is one great certainty: each and every one of us will die, probably this side of a hundred years, probably well this side of a hundred years. The older we get, the faster the years go by and, with increasing age, the transience of the physical frame becomes undeniable.

Bodily existence is transient and yet we spend a large proportion of our time working to support and nurture it. Sometimes it seems that we are obsessed by acquiring things, whether necessary for existence or not. We spend our time inventing gadgets, indulging in hobbies or sports or socialising, though we know all these things will end, sooner or later. If we accept that such interests are normal, valuable in their own way, but limited solely to the material side of life, is there anything more lasting? If we do not want to live forever, or to 'take it with us when we go', what is there that might outlast purely material existence?

We have only the moment, now, in which we live. Is there anything here we can capture? Is there anything in momentary experience that we can grasp at and somehow make our own? There is not. The mind and matter of the moment is so transient it is gone before we can even register its presence.

Whether we imagine the lives of solar systems, empires, individuals or moments, all of them are transient. Nothing lasts. Death claims all. All is transient.

We need the meditation to bring insight into transience home to us in real experience rather than purely as an intellectual exercise. Of the five factors necessary to progress on the path, insight into transience is critical. To develop insight in the meditation we need to become aware through direct experience that things are transient, so transient that they disappear mere moments after they arise. It is not enough to attend to conventional things like relationships, houses, cars and people. We need to attend to the ultimates of experience such as feelings or sensory consciousness, to the very building-blocks of experience. Only then can insight into transience, unsatisfactoriness and non-self arise.

* * *

The last of the factors essential for progress is a reliable source of guidance. If you belong to the middle band of seekers who are able to attain enlightenment only with assistance, then a good teacher is a necessity.

There are many fine teachers in the world today. Studying with them could provide the support for a meditator to generate the insight necessary to progress towards enlightenment. There are often problems to be overcome, however. A teacher may not speak the same language as the student. Climate may be a problem. The instruction, though excellent, may not suit the particular meditator.

The crux of the matter is whether the student's mindfulness increases under the guidance of the teacher he has chosen. If it does not, no matter how famous, knowledgeable, experienced, kind or understanding the teacher may be, the student should leave as quickly as possible in search of a teacher who, for him, is better.

When you do find a teacher under whose instruction your mindfulness increases then, even if you find him or the conditions difficult to get on with, you should stay as long as you can. The Buddha himself said that if you find circumstances—a place, support, teaching—under which your mindfulness improves, thus opening the way to progress, you should stay with them, even if it is difficult to do so.

I have placed the teacher last in the equation for a very good reason. The most important of the five factors is the desire to find the truth, which itself grows out of insight into suffering. The process is circular: right view is both the beginning and the end of the noble eightfold path. The more insight into suffering there is, the more desire and urgency; the greater the desire, the more insight into suffering.

When the desire to find truth is strongly based on insight, we get the curious case of a student who *cannot* be damaged by his circumstances, for he turns everything to good account in his search for truth and freedom. Sometimes, for example, a student of this calibre will unwittingly seek instruction from a bad teacher. No matter what the teacher does or says, the student views those things in the light of his own greater understanding. Doing so, he learns—and his insight deepens. You could say that, whatever his circumstances, he learns from life itself.

It is more common to find a poor student with a good teacher. In this case, the student manages to perceive in the teacher only the reflections of his or her own inexperienced mind. Viewing the world through his own misunderstandings, the student may falsely ascribe ulterior motives or vicious states of mind to the teacher, being unable to contemplate anything else.

The Buddha asked his monks, 'Can a bad man know a good man?' Rightly, the monks replied, 'No, Sir.' The Buddha continued, 'Can a good man know a bad man?' The monks replied, 'Yes, certainly.'

Why is this? Think of it in terms of a skill you might possess. The skill in question could be almost anything: typing, music, glassblowing or mathematical ability. Can you identify someone who does not have that skill? Can you identify someone who does? How do you know? You recognise, or fail to find, the marks of relevant experience in the other person. You may have to ask a few questions, or ask for a demonstration, but you quickly discover the truth.

If you have developed the skill of living by restraint, you know the pitfalls of craving, hatred and selfish indulgence for yourself. Can you identify someone who is unrestrained, who has not learned the benefits of ethical conduct and forbearance? Of course you can. In the past, you yourself acted in that way and suffered the consequences. You know the problems. You know the pitfalls. You can easily recognise the actions you once performed and the kinds of results that ensued. It is no mystery.

On the other hand, the person who has never considered restraint cannot recognise someone who lives by it. Someone who indulges every selfish whim, who has no concept of the benefits of curtailing those actions that distress or harm other beings, has no basis from which to assess harmless people. Looking at others, he projects on to them only his own motives, being unable to recognise any other. A bad man cannot know a good man.

It is said that when the student is ready the teacher will appear— one of those intriguing aphorisms that, on examination, could mean many things. I take it to mean that a student, seeking someone to answer his questions, can recognise an individual who has gained insight into the problems with which he is still struggling. Put another way, when we have enough knowledge and experience to ask the right questions, it is easier to know who might help us find the answers.

Finding the answers is never easy. Even under ideal circumstances a great deal depends upon the individual student's level of desire and insight. Indeed, the balance for an individual of the five factors of desire for truth, freedom from external hindrances, freedom from internal hindrances, insight and guidance will determine his rate of progress on the path. If these are strong then he is likely to travel quickly towards total freedom from distress, towards the highest bliss, towards the total transcendence of the world. If they are weak, then progress is likely to be halting and unsteady.

Abilities vary. We are not all equal on the search for truth and freedom. Only a tiny minority of people can attain the goal without any guidance. Those who do, but cannot teach, the Buddha called *pacceka* Buddhas, silent Buddhas. Members of another small minority, at the other end of the spectrum, have insuperable obstacles, usually resulting from past actions of an extremely inefficient nature, that prevent any progress in this lifetime. The majority of us, those between the extremes, need help and guidance.

The best supporting conditions for the struggle towards the light are to be found by entering the Order as a monk or nun but, even with otherwise perfect conditions, an effective teacher is a necessity. The two combined provide a very powerful environment.

A suitable teacher may be essential but, even if one is found, the student is the one who has to do the work; the teacher 'can but point the way'. Everyone who walks the path does so as a pioneer, making unique discoveries for himself. The whole point of learning from experience is that no one else can do it for us. The map of the teaching is not the territory. Each student is an explorer intent on finding out for himself what lies behind appearances.

Eventually, after many personal trials and much hard work, a student can attain the goal of the meditative life. Then, student no longer, he can say with all those who preceded him, 'Done is that which had to be done. For this, there is no more becoming.'

Having come this far, there is no further to go. The journey of lifetimes is finally at an end and there is only understanding and peace. Suffering has been overcome and the burden put down. There is no more need to search.

15

This Fathom-Long Carcase

The Buddha said: 'I will show you the arising and passing away of the world within this fathom-long carcase.'

All we can be aware of—the world—ultimately comes down to what we can sense, internally and externally. No matter what theories of the world there may be, all have eventually to be tested against direct experience through the five physical senses and the mind. So, our entire experience, the universe itself, consists of six internal and six external sense-fields.

The internal sense-fields are eye, ear, nose, tongue, body and mind. The external sense-fields are shape-and-colour, sound, smell, taste, touch and mental objects. The sense-fields, internal and external, contain the arising and passing away of this whole vast universe. None of the physical sense-fields cross over—the ear cannot see, the eye cannot hear—but the information they provide is woven together in the mind.

The Buddha summarised his teaching in the four noble truths: there is suffering, there is a cause of suffering, there is the cessation of suffering and there is a way leading to the cessation of suffering.

The first truth seems obvious at one level: it is difficult to ignore the distress in the world, whether internal or external. From the horrors of war and famine, and the threat of plague, to personal disasters of poverty, homelessness, disease, cancer, rape and robbery. When we add to these the agonies of the mental universe—fear, grief, sorrow, frustration, despair and depression—the picture is complete: there is suffering in the world. Many people fear for their lives and welfare. Recent news of 'flesh-eating bacteria' terrified many. Currently, issues surrounding the disposal of radioactive waste are arousing strong passions even in the usually most mild-mannered.

We all know about suffering, at least in its obvious forms. We may even be aware of the unsatisfactory nature of the good times as well; they are so fleeting, they take so much work to get and maintain. They too are *dukkha*, suffering. But are we aware of the reason for this state of affairs? Do we know why we find life as unsatisfactory as we do? If we have thought about it at all, we may have concluded that there is no pattern to disaster—it just seems to strike at random.

Tonight I want to look at the second noble truth: there is a cause of suffering.

Some people find it hard to believe that suffering has an identifiable cause, thinking that the world is an assemblage of chance events. Others will allow a material cause for distress, believing, for example, that every disease is due to some kind of pathogen and that every discomfort stems from material poverty. Unlike the Buddha and his followers, these individuals do not consider the mind to be a significant factor.

The Buddha stated unequivocally that there is a *cause* of suffering; there is a reason for it. It is not due to chance; it is not due to 'bad luck'. The reason for suffering lies not in poverty, bacteria, pathogens or oppression by our enemies, but within us.

The cause of suffering is craving, *tanhā*. But what is craving? We use the word easily enough, but do we really understand it? Craving or greed is wanting desperately to have something. It leads to mental and physical grasping at this and that, always with the aim of acquisition. When relentlessly repeated, grasping becomes attachment: clinging on with refusal to relinquish. According to the Buddha's teaching, craving and attachment are responsible for all the suffering in the world.

What do we want so much? What are the things we lust after? They are the six internal and external sense-fields, for there is nothing else. We desire to acquire things we do not have, or to get rid of things we find unpleasant.

Internally, personally, we may wish that our own physical sense organs were perfect, that they were not affected by ageing and decay, not damaged by infection or accident. We desire fitness and health, youth and vitality. We may opt for plastic surgery, or undergo strenuous workouts to ward off the flab. Perhaps we yearn to be sophisticated and try to educate our ears to music considered good and our palates to the tastes of fine foods and drinks. Some pride themselves on their sense of smell, others on having little or none at all. We seek all manner of sensitivities in the physical sense organs.

When we examine the mind, the consciousness that measures the internal and external worlds, we find that here too we desire to shape and adjust ourselves. We may hanker always to be well-informed perhaps or, if life is getting us down, we may crave oblivion and try to dull the mind with drink or drugs, with fantasy or ignorance. Some, conscious of widespread distress, yearn for a mind that can pierce the veils hiding reality and practise prayer or meditation for that purpose.

The physical things we crave for externally cover the whole of material existence. They include sensual indulgence of all sorts, from food to our neighbours' land and property. There is no physical thing that has not been a positive or negative object of desire.

When we come to mental objects, the list is even more extensive, for we may desire anything whatsoever—past or present, real or imaginary, near or far, rational or irrational, mental or physical. A mental object may be an image of a hedonistic utopia, or the idea of gaining perfect concentration or even enlightenment itself. So we thirst for things mental and physical and it is this craving and attachment that the Buddha defined as the cause of suffering.

Why are the results of craving so terrible? How does it produce the torment we are all familiar with? Our actions, driven by craving, are the force, the *kamma*, that brings about the unsatisfactory results. We form a picture or a concept of something we want and then worry at it like a dog with a bone, always seeking to find how we might possess it. We convince ourselves that it is vital to our well-being, that we cannot live without it. If we cannot acquire the object of our desire, we fall into depression and life seems worthless. All this is suffering.

Even when we manage to get what we want we are sooner or later disappointed. Either it is quite different in reality from our imagined picture, in which case we feel cheated, or it does not last as long as we would wish and, again, we feel cheated. Our actions resonate into the future, even into future lives. Echoes of past deeds, past cravings and hatreds, follow us down through the centuries even on to other planes of existence.

Here are just some of the ways in which we bring disaster down on our heads. Craving power or property, we make war on others.

Through hatred or insecurity, we persecute and kill those with different religious or political beliefs. We fight our neighbours over trivial disagreements. We pursue fierce power struggles in the office and seek to dominate our partners in the home.

If making war is one favourite pastime, the 'game of love' is surely the next most popular. Craving love and relationship, we steal another's partner or seek clandestine affairs. For excitement, for titillation, for 'true love', for endless reasons and excuses we play the game in all its many variations, often to our own and others' detriment.

Craving wealth and possessions, we steal or defraud; we 'forget' to return a borrowed book or tool; we move the garden fence a few inches into our neighbour's territory; we go shoplifting, or creep around in the dark stealing others' possessions. We set up fraudulent companies that accept money but never provide goods or services; we defraud pension funds or embezzle company funds. Politicians make international war, either for power or to steal the resources of their neighbours. The list goes on and on.

Craving fame and recognition, we turn to the entertainment industry or to politics. Sometimes we try to buy favour with money, if we have it, or services, if we do not. Most of us know someone who can always be relied on to find exactly the thing, person or piece of information we need in return for our friendship.

When such activities are driven by craving and attachment, they lead to immediate suffering. Lusting after anything at all breeds intense dissatisfaction. Making war, whether by word or deed, brings distress to all touched by the activity. If you even occasionally see the television news, you cannot escape pictures of extreme hardship and suffering brought about by warfare or terrorism.

Activities recognisably criminal bring with them the real threat of punishment, while those merely anti-social carry an overhead in terms of fear and anxiety for the perpetrator. Long-term results could be horrific. The Pali Canon tells us that those who indulge in great craving may be destined for a bad rebirth in the next life, even for rebirth into one of the many hell states that Buddhism recognises.

Those in the majority who do not indulge themselves excessively nevertheless still find themselves tied to the wheel of *samsāra*, destined for another birth, destined therefore for all of the sufferings that attend another birth, life and death. Many of us have no wish to go through the agonising trials of childhood or adolescence again.

Why do we do it? Why do we pursue craving and attachment when their outcome is invariably unsatisfactory at the very least, and at the worst vile, painful, damaging to ourselves and hurtful to others?

We do these things because we do not perceive the truth. We believe, wrongly, that the different things we yearn for—power, wealth, fame, possessions and relationships—will give us the satisfaction or happiness that we long for, in spite of all the evidence to the contrary.

Most of us chase after things that, while pleasing in the short term, can never ultimately give us what we want. We do not realise that this craving, which many people consider perfectly acceptable and even desirable, is the cause of all distress. We are blind to the truth of things, blind to the four noble truths. This current inability to see is the blindness (*avijjā*) of which the Buddha spoke and which lies behind any craving or attachment. Craving is possible only when there is blindness or ignorance of the true nature of the world.

Suffering is a symptom of severe imbalance, of expending our energies in counter-productive directions dictated by craving. How do we bring our lives into a harmonious balance with reality? How do we stop ourselves indulging in the craving and attachment that produce future anguish for us? One might think that we would learn through our mistakes, but that is clearly not the case as things stand, for we are literally blind to the damage we do.

Somehow, we have to undo the blindness and learn to see what is actually taking place. If we develop the capacity to observe dispassionately, we will see that the things we set so much store by are truly not capable of giving us what we seek. Our control over them is largely illusory: they arise and cease quickly, and grasping at them produces deep anguish. Only if we *experience* through direct observation the fact that the world is insubstantial, not lasting, will we be convinced of our error. Thought or intellectual understanding alone can never solve the problems for us.

* * *

The things we love and hate are all within the six sensory fields, for there is nothing outside of them. Anything we can imagine, anything we can experience, is likewise within the six sensory fields that are constantly arising and passing away. In fact, things are not nearly so lasting as they ordinarily appear. When seen clearly, 'the world' arises moment by moment, with contact between sense and object. It does not exist other than through that contact.

To see and comprehend the moment-by-moment arising and ceasing of all that we normally rely upon, we must tackle the problem systematically. The very best way of doing this is to follow the instructions the Buddha laid down in the eightfold path. The eight components of the path are right view, right thought, right speech, right action, right livelihood, right effort, right mindfulness and right concentration. They fall naturally into three divisions: *sīla*, or discipline; *samādhi*, or mindfulness and concentration; and *paññā*, or wisdom.

Sīla is the restraint of overt actions driven by craving and attachment, or selfishness. For the lay person, this restraint is usually accomplished by following the guidelines of the five precepts. For recluses, there are many more rules.

Samādhi is the restraint of more subtle cravings and attachments, through developing sense-restraint, mindfulness and control, to arrive at deeply concentrated states of mind unhindered by sensual impacts or mental distractions.

Paññā, experiential wisdom, is generated from the observation and experience of the six internal and six external sense-fields at the momentary level. Specifically, it is the wisdom gained from direct observation of the transience of all things.

Systematically developing mindfulness and concentration allows us to see the processes of mind more clearly. Increasingly accurate observation of the six internal and six external sense-fields ultimately shows us that every aspect of them is disappearing instant by instant. Insight meditation proves at the subjective, personal/emotional level that the so-called 'things' we hunger for and are so attached to, whether material or mental, are so fleeting that there is truly nothing there to get hold of, much less to keep. We become able see our intentions to act, the grasping at this and that, and the results that follow from those actions.

Insight meditation sheds light on the true nature of the momentary occurrence of things. For example, when we look at a person, a tree, a mountain, a face or a work of art, just what do we see? At the ultimate, fundamental level, we see only shape and colour. How long does it last? It lasts only an instant. In fact, if you analyse how the eye and the mind build up a picture, you will find that what we so confidently identify as a 'thing' is actually a composite made up of many small scans of the eye over an appreciable period of time. To make a picture of a tree or a person, the mind brings together information drawn through the 'eye-door' at different times, all of it slightly out of date, all of it at one remove from the actual experience of seeing.

What is really there? All we can prove is that momentary shape and colour arise, last for an instant and then disappear. Anything else is added by the mind and is of questionable accuracy. At the level of conventional truth, we may be looking at a friend we have known for years. This perception is perfectly valid in its own sphere, the conventional world, but is false and misleading from the ultimate point of view. Ultimately speaking, all there is in the act of seeing is the apprehension of shape and colour. There follows a discriminative process, perception, alerting us to the conventional interpretation of the raw data just apprehended. Interpretation is unavoidably biased and partial and is likewise inevitably based on past data. It belongs to the conventional universe and, as such, cannot be relied upon. Once we start to deal in perceptions, we start to deal in personal opinions— and those are notoriously fickle.

It is, of course, in the mind, in the mental arena, where most of the difficulties arise. It is convenient to divide experience into body and mind but, in the last analysis, the mind is the more important of the two as it adds the apparent value to an object.

What is a mental object? It may be anything at all, real or imaginary, but let us take as an example an image of success. Maybe someone craves to be successful—at work, in the theatre, in the arts, in meditation—it really does not matter. The idea of success arises most probably as a mental picture. Examined with the eye of meditative attention, the mental image is seen to arise, persist for a moment and then disappear. It disappears in one of a number of ways: it may diminish in size and wink out; it may drift off to the left or right of the mental visual field; it may fragment or thin out and fade away.

The point at issue is that it does always disappear—quickly. It is not possible to make the image last. True, one can create another image of success, but it is a different one, and that too will be as transient as the last. When mindfulness and concentration are strong and this process is seen clearly, you will see that mental images present themselves with extreme rapidity; they come and go almost instantaneously, rather like the frames of a movie film.

If we gain success in the world itself, we find that also is transient, even at the relative, worldly level. Of course, it appears to last much longer than the mental object but, when examined closely, turns out to be no different. It, like everything else, is composed of discrete sensory experiences, all of which are momentary in nature.

★ ★ ★

How does suffering arise? How is the 'danger in the world', suffering, caused by craving? Suffering arises when, craving for or lusting after this or that, we attempt to hold on to things and to manipulate events into a permanent pattern. We attempt to create what we long for out of components as ephemeral as soap bubbles. It is like trying to write on water or to build castles in the air. We can never succeed, so we experience frustration and anguish. Further, we condition ourselves to future distress for the blind efforts we make resonate through future lifetimes, bringing us painful rebirths and difficult personal circumstances.

Seeing how utterly insubstantial things are, internally and externally, it becomes overwhelmingly obvious that it is literally impossible to grasp successfully at anything. Seeing transience so clearly destroys craving and attachment for all time. Thus is the task completed, the end of suffering found.

We discover for a fact what we all suspect deep down: we are beings of light and love. We do not need any artifice to be happy and free from anguish for we are already free. We have only to wake up. We have only to melt away the confusion and the blindness to discover the freedom and love that are always there. We do not have to create freedom. We do not have to create love. They are eternally present, waiting undiminished for each of us to wake up and learn to love the light.

The Buddha said, 'I will show you the arising and passing away of the world within this fathom-long carcase.' For those who are troubled and ill at ease, there is a way out. The way out is the Buddha's eightfold path that enables us to overcome the craving upon which all distress arises. The necessary steps are self-discipline through the precepts, self-restraint through concentration and the setting up of systematic mindfulness, and the overcoming of ignorance of the way things really are through developing the special meditation on transience.

Experiencing the momentary transience of every aspect of the six internal and six external sense-fields undercuts craving, cuts it off, renders it extinct, thus eliminating the very root of all anguish. This is enlightenment, *nibbāna*, the goal of the Buddha's path to the deathless.

16

The Ultimate Security

All human beings strive for three things: security, fulfilment and power. We strive for security or permanence; we strive for fulfilment or satisfaction; and we strive for power, self-aggrandisement, ownership and control. To these ends, we are prepared to exert ourselves heroically. We sacrifice freedom for security, reputation for fulfilment and self-respect for power, such is the grip these things have on us.

Tonight I want to look at security. Why do we desire it so? What actually is it? How do we best invest our time and effort to get it?

Security is safety—imagined safety, it has to be said—for the foreseeable future. It takes several forms.

Material security is the assurance or likelihood of maintained or increasing health, wealth, ownership and employment. As something we strive for, it could be freedom from poverty, illness and disease.

We also desire emotional security. We seek out a compatible partner and friends. We want our emotional life to be rich, varied and deeply satisfying. Perversely, some of us shun the unpredictability of human beings and seek our emotional security in work, in columns of figures or in problem-solving, scared always of being vulnerable and getting hurt.

Sometimes we try to avoid vulnerability, insecurity, by adopting particular mental attitudes. We seek intellectual comfort through the views we choose to hold and seek out only those who agree with us. Those of us with similar shades of political, religious or any other opinion tend to collect together, thereby affirming each other's worth.

On the television some while ago, there was programme about a young British Asian who had gone to Northern Ireland. In Belfast, she was asked by a girl she met whether she was a Catholic or a Protestant. She said, smiling, 'I'm a Hindu.' There was a long silence, and then her new friend said, 'Yes, but are you a Catholic Hindu or a Protestant Hindu?'

We cling to the security of our views.

Many people believe in Science and Technology, the twin gods of the modern age, and some believe that they promise a universal solution to the problem of uncertainty. These new deities will heal all ills, ensure prosperity and become the basis for longer life. They will solve every mystery, cure every ill and replace every broken heart with a transplant. If life should become incurably dull, science and technology will provide us with a more exciting substitute by way of virtual reality.

We strive to feel secure, and grasp strongly at some or all of these things. In doing so, we place our trust in things that cannot give us what we want. What happens to material and mental security when there is war or conflict? News reports show us just how ephemeral material security can be. From the countless reports of the war in Bosnia Herzegovina, one particular image has stayed with me. It was of a once beautiful, small country farmhouse in a delightful setting, but now with its roof stove in and derelict. It was easy to imagine an ordinary family living there comfortably and happily, their 'secure' lifestyle shattered in a few moments of violence and terror.

We do not have to go so far afield to become aware of insecurity. The ills of recession are all around us. Over recent months I have met many people who have been made redundant or who have had their houses repossessed, who have lost everything and are now forced to scrape a hand-to-mouth living in this, the prosperous West. In such times, the much relied-upon insurance often does not pay up. Nothing is ultimately capable of protecting us against change.

Even if financially secure, we are not safe, for no amount of wealth or insurance can prevent sickness and death. Even if we escape some of the common killers like cancer or heart disease, we can remain healthy only for a limited time. It is rarely that someone lives past one hundred years of age and I have heard of no one older than one hundred and ten.

However strong man's material safeguards, however robust his health, the forces of nature are always the stronger. The British Isles are tilting, sinking in the east and rising in the west. Eastern coastal sea defences are gradually being overwhelmed and, in the long term, nothing can be done to halt the incursion of the sea. Coastal erosion is a problem and, at Scarborough, an entire cliff-top hotel has slipped into the sea. On the south coast, near Beachy Head, the owners spent a small fortune moving their whole house back on rails from the approaching cliff edge. In London, the technological marvel of the Thames Barrier has so far prevented flooding, but for how much longer?

There is no lasting material security and, where mental security depends on external things, there can be no lasting mental security either. When disaster strikes, the majority falls into despair. No matter how much time and money we invest in safeguards, they cannot provide cast-iron security.

Realising the unreliable nature of the world, many of us seek security through some kind of religious or spiritual quest. Some try to maximise their chances of salvation by joining as many different religious or spiritual groups as possible. Others believe that an occasional appearance at a spiritual gathering will do the trick. A few give huge donations to charity to buy a place in heaven. Others are armchair seekers who read a great deal but never put into practice what they learn. A few commit themselves completely to practising the way of their choice.

I suppose the majority of people put their faith either in science or in the teachings of a religious way. Whatever you choose, there are benefits and there are dangers. It is entirely possible to pick up a belief system in completely the wrong way. This can lead to what we might call wrong certainty, or wrong emotional security. Wrong certainty is greatly to be feared. It leads to the closed mind and to the worst excesses man can devise. It can lead to all kinds of dogmatism and bigotry. Desperately wanting to be secure but not knowing how, some grasp fanatically at the teachings of their chosen way, be it science or religion, materialism or humanism, new age philosophies or whatever else. They dare not question too deeply for that would be to admit their own confusion, and the uncertainty would be hard to bear.

If you adopt views that are wrong, there is at least the consolation that you damage only yourself in the process. Some, however, take it much further. Convinced that their way is the only one, they try to force everyone else to adopt it, like the drunkard who always presses others to drink with him. It is as though they think that, if enough people believe in something, it must be true. With missionary fervour, they proselytise their neighbours and may even travel abroad to spread the message they believe in so strongly. In extreme cases, this kind of activity can severely damage other people, even as far as causing their deaths.

In the Crusades, hundreds of thousands of men went to fight in foreign lands in the cause of religion. Later, the Spanish Inquisition performed terrible deeds under the guise of 'what is best for people'. In such instances, reason and logic seem to be in short supply; fanatical belief is the order of the day. Bizarre practices become respected and superstition is elevated to the status of undeniable truth. Witchcraft trials were a case in point.

One test to find the supposed guilt or innocence of witches was ordeal by water. Hands and feet tied, the accused, usually a woman, was lowered into water. If innocent, she sank, being 'accepted' by the pure water. Some victims drowned or, if elderly, died from the shock of the cold water, this being taken as evidence of guilt. If she floated, if the water 'rejected' her, this proved her guilt—and the unfortunate woman survived the ordeal only to be burned at the stake. Unsurprisingly, there were many proven-to-be-guilty victims. In our own day, atrocities like ethnic cleansing are always prosecuted in the name of a belief system, often a belief system with a religious footing.

★ ★ ★

All these kinds of problems existed in the Buddha's day. Just as today, people strove for security, fulfilment and power. Then, just as now, they sought certainty and security in innumerable ways: science, wealth, power, commerce and banditry, soothsaying, palmistry, astrology and religion. There were dogmatists and missionaries, zealots and sincere hard-working people just as there are today.

There does seem to have been one significant difference, however, in that there appears to have been greater understanding in those days of the overall pattern of the world. The commentaries to the Pali Canon tell us that the science of the day recognised five great natural orders (*niyāma*). Each was a distinct area of study and was understood to have its own laws.

There was the natural order of the physical world, which is the basis of science as we know it, and the natural order of the life of plants, or botany. Then came the natural order of action and result (the law of *kamma*), which states that selfish actions of body, speech and mind lead to suffering whereas unselfish actions of body, speech and mind lead to growing happiness. There was the natural order of mind, which includes the laws governing all aspects of mind and mental states, including the deepest levels of concentration, psychic powers and their component processes. And then there was the natural order of the lives of Buddhas, a body of laws governing when and how frequently a Buddha might appear in the world.

While the first two broadly describe science as we know it today, the last three are still largely unknown in the West. For example, the existence of an actual law governing the results of ethical actions seems fanciful to most, in spite of a call for more morality from those in positions of authority. The idea that we condition our own future happiness and distress by the actions we perform seems literally incredible to many modern scientific minds.

The teaching of the Buddha is rendered even more difficult for some Westerners because of its insistence on rebirth from life to life. Not only do our actions affect us later in this life, but they also affect our destiny in the next. What is more, there is not just one more life, but an uncountable number. At birth, we bring with us all kinds of conditioning from countless past lives. We have created the very conditions in which we presently find ourselves and as such cannot blame anyone else for them.

On the question of mind, many Westerners do not believe that psychic powers even exist, let alone that there are laws governing every aspect of mind and mental behaviour. We tend to be very sceptical. As for the circumstances surrounding the appearance of Buddhas, that is so far outside what most consider reasonable as to be beyond comment.

For our own safety and security, we have to learn about the world in which we live. We have to learn how safely to cross a road. We have to learn the rules of social interaction so that we may live harmoniously in a community. We have to learn skills so that we can earn money to live. We are learning all the time.

Through the education system, our early teachers seek to provide us with a broad mix of skills that enable us to take our places in the community. What seems to be missing, though, is any instruction in what is truly best for ourselves and for others. To include this would mean going beyond reading and writing, beyond woodwork and kitchen science, beyond languages and the arts and most certainly beyond science and technology. As things stand, we can gain the missing features through independent study, and we are fortunate in having books and teachers readily available should we be interested enough to look.

For best results, we need at least a working understanding of *kamma* and *vipāka*, action and result. For a more rounded picture, we need to recognise that there is not just the one life, as many would claim, but so many that our existence is better described as 'an endless faring on' (*samsāra*). While becoming intellectually conversant with these things is valuable in itself, we gain most benefit from acting on what we learn. We have to apply the knowledge that the exercise of greed and hatred will harm not only others but ourselves in the future. When we do act with this in mind, and restrain personal greed and hatred, we find many very real benefits from right view and right action.

The rewards of right view and right action are extensive. Generosity leads to prosperity. Forbearance and unselfishness lead to happiness. Self-restraint brings peace of mind. Good actions of all kinds lead to a rebirth in either a fortunate human state or in other realms more pleasant still. The practice of loving-kindness brings harmony, contentment, popularity and freedom from danger.

The principle behind these laws seems at first to turn common-sense on its head. How can you become prosperous by giving things away? How can you enjoy yourself by restraining sensual desire? It does not make sense according to the materialistic view to which most of us are accustomed. And yet it works and we can prove that it works. Observing our own behaviour, we can prove for ourselves that selfishness really does breed sorrow and unselfishness quite definitely leads to well-being and happiness.

Investment in unselfish actions brings a security very much more reliable than that found through investing only in material things. The kind of security that is based on material wealth is greatly affected by changing world markets, tariffs, politics, unemployment and recession; it is limited and never completely secure. In contrast, unselfish actions depend on a much more subtle and powerful law, the law of *kamma*, which applies right across all the worlds of *samsāra* to the outermost reaches of physical and mental phenomena. The results of action can never be taken away from the individual. Further, knowing that we have performed actions that will have pleasant resultants provides a deep sense of security for the future.

* * *

According to Buddhist cosmology, *samsāra* is divided into thirty-one worlds, or planes, of which there are four where greater suffering is experienced than in the human realm and twenty-six where life is more pleasant, even delightful. Our ethical actions—our *kamma*—predispose us after death to be born on one or another of these planes, dependent upon whether they have been skilful or unskilful.

The worlds more painful than the human realm are collectively known as 'the woeful way'. Entering them is to embark on lifetimes of pain and anguish. Those more pleasant are described as 'the happy destiny' and offer lifetimes of ease and relative freedom from major distress. The human realm is unique in having a roughly equal balance of pleasure and pain.

All the worlds, without exception, are subject to conditions. In ultimate terms, they are transient, unsatisfactory and non-self. Though the pleasant realms of existence are long-lasting, conventionally speaking, in the last analysis they are unsatisfactory, *dukkha*, precisely because there is no chance whatever of experiencing them permanently. Every aspect of them is transient, and that is sufficient to reject them as a final answer to suffering and distress.

None of the wonderful gains from right action is ultimately secure, in this life or another, for by their very nature they cannot last. To acquire more of the same needs constant selfless work. Good results have constantly to be worked for, to be engineered and maintained, if they are to continue.

For ultimate security, we must look beyond even the happy states, beyond even unselfish action, and for this we need to learn about the higher truth.

* * *

The higher aim of the Buddha's teaching is to end all suffering and insecurity. The Buddha expounded the essence of his teaching in the four noble truths. He said that suffering and insecurity are universal and unavoidable experiences that exist everywhere within the relative worlds. He said that suffering has a cause, that it does not arise without reason. That cause, or major condition, is craving based on ignorance of the true nature of reality. He also categorically stated the existence of *nibbāna*, freedom from suffering, the end of insecurity, and identified it as the only true escape from *samsāra*. In the fourth noble truth he laid out in detail the path leading to the cessation of all distress, the path to total security and freedom from suffering.

The way to the goal of freedom depends on a foundation of ethical action. Ethical action provides the necessary stability of mind and mental states to allow us to set up mindfulness and concentration. Once the mind is free from hindrances, is purified, we can then practise insight meditation. Insight meditation is to become aware by experience of the fact that all things arise and fall. No matter how large, no matter how small, no matter how long-term, no matter how short-term, all things arise and fall. Insight meditation is to become aware through direct experience that all relative things are transient. In the process, the meditator also becomes aware that all relative things are unsatisfactory and that all things—including the state of freedom itself (*nibbāna*)—are non-self.

When describing the true nature of the world, the Buddha would say, 'This law of nature prevails: namely, all phenomena are transient. This law of nature prevails: namely, all phenomena are unsatisfactory. This law of nature prevails: namely, all phenomena are non-self.' If they are transient and non-self, they are uncontrollable, cannot be owned and most certainly cannot be relied upon. He emphasised that all mundane things, physical and mental, gross and fine, are subject to these laws. It is therefore impossible that anything mundane could provide a foundation for lasting security.

The Buddha's teaching has but one aim: to eradicate all insecurity, to eliminate all suffering. For this, we have to overturn ignorance through cultivating wisdom. Insight wisdom is attained by gaining experiential certainty, through meditation, that all compounded things are transient and unsatisfactory, and all things whatever, including the end of all distress and insecurity, are without self.

The ultimate and most reliable investment of time and effort lies in the practice of what the Buddha taught. The eightfold path leads to the higher truth that allows us to realise the ultimate security, total freedom from rebirth, total freedom from suffering and distress.

This is a far more valuable goal than to seek material possessions, satisfaction of the senses or power. It is more worthwhile than seeking the rewards of selfless action. The gains from following the way of the Buddha successfully are beyond price, incalculable.

Some see the task as endless, as impossibly difficult. It is not. Meditation is not indulging in a hazy, imprecise and fuzzy dream. The meditation practice is governed by natural laws, as definite as those found in modern science. If we practise rightly, we must reach the end of the road. Success rests upon the systematic development of mindfulness and concentration, together with clear comprehension applied to what we do. These tasks are well within the abilities of most people, should they wish to make the effort.

The task is manageable. It is entirely possible today, just as it was in the Buddha's time. It all depends upon how we approach it. The Buddha said, 'Whosoever eats, drinks, munches and crunches must answer the calls of nature: such is the issue of it. He who pays attention to the rising and falling of things must come to the cessation of suffering: such is the issue of it.'

Practising in this way, a growing certainty will develop that you are destined for complete freedom. There arises a totally unshakeable confidence, founded upon experience, that you will come to know what is currently still unknown to you. This is not an illusion, nor is it possible to mistake it for one. You know, and that is all there is to it. The arising of this knowledge marks the certainty, the total security, of those who have won to the stream, streamwinners. Such individuals, even if they stop working at the meditation, will become enlightened within a maximum of seven lifetimes. With continued application, a meditator can greatly reduce that delay, even to becoming enlightened and totally secure within this very lifetime. It is definitely still possible today, just as it ever was. The path is there. All you have to do is walk it.

17

The Quiet Mind

I want to describe the kind of mind that results from successfully walking the meditative path. I will try to give you a flavour, as it were, of the goal. But first, a word of caution, for any description of the beyond is bound to be inadequate and should not be taken too seriously. Enlightenment, the cessation of suffering, is beyond logic, beyond definition and completely beyond the relative world; any terms applied are necessarily inaccurate. My intention is to convey a hint of something about which nothing accurate can ever be said.

It will be least inaccurate to start by listing things that are left behind when the goal is attained. Enlightenment is the destruction and subsequent absence of ignorance, craving and hatred. It is the elimination of suffering in its many forms. Enlightenment is freedom from guilt, from self-pity, from aggression, from attachment of any description and from the threat of future birth and death. In the absence of these disturbances, the mind is quiet.

The quiet mind is quiet because there is no expectation; it does not expect things to occur—or not to occur—but lives moment by moment. It will still make plans, when necessary. There are many things that need some foresight: shopping lists, routes for long car journeys, menus for a week when visitors are staying, and many other similar activities. Making a plan, however, is not at all the same thing as expecting that plan to work in every particular. The shop may be out of stock of some things, roadworks may demand a detour, when visitors are staying you may decide to eat out sometimes. For the quiet mind, this is not a problem, for all plans are necessarily tentative; there is always another alternative. When there is no attachment, 'failure' is not an issue and certainly not a major problem.

While some people become greatly distressed owing to their expectation that everything should go exactly as planned, most of us have no difficulty with plans going awry at this mundane level. An area where many more of us do experience problems, however, is that of major life changes. We may spend hours, days and weeks distressed by attempts to come to a decision about what we should do. Here, too, the quiet mind is free from concern. There is no worry about what direction one's life will take nor expectation about the results of, say, a job interview or a promotion. There is no concern about how one might react to failing health, to redundancy, to divorce, to moving house, to dying. Expectations of this kind are completely absent from the quiet mind.

In case it should appear that the quiet mind basks in a sort of tranquil never-never-land, I should mention that enlightenment changes nothing except the occurrence of ignorance, craving and hatred. Understanding the four noble truths does not thereby confer mundane expertise, and the individual is left much as before in terms of his or her set of skills and preferences. Some in training may be social, gregarious and out-going, fond of company and naturally expansive. Others, in complete contrast, may prefer their own company and choose to lead much less social lives. These preferences do not change with realisation of the goal. In a similar vein, if an individual in training is a skilled teacher, say, he remains so, and one with no aptitude in this direction does not magically acquire it. Just as one would not expect suddenly to acquire the ability to speak Swahili if unable to beforehand, so too does one not gain other mundane skills.

Hope is another form of expectation absent from the quiet mind. My teacher used to say that—if it wasn't for the fact that it would have been misconstrued—he would have had carved into the stone-work above the door of the monastery the legend, 'Abandon hope all ye who enter here.' The absence of hope is, contrary to the popular view, a very positive state.

Dreams, too, are absent. Whether self-aggrandising fantasies, or the kinds of dreams described as 'building castles in the air', they have no place in the mind freed from the noise and stink of suffering that comes about dependent on craving and ignorance.

Ignorance in one of its aspects is a volitional activity that we do to avoid discomfort or a potential problem—we ignore what we have no wish to deal with, whether internal or external. We have come to think of ignorance as unawareness. To some degree, that is of course the case; ignorance has become so habitual that it is often no longer a conscious activity. But ask yourselves *how* we ignore something. First, we become aware of it and only then—when we know what it is— do we decide to pay it no further attention, to ignore it. We ignore either the object itself or, more commonly, certain *qualities* of the object. For instance, we know that the body is mortal—it will inexorably decay and die usually well within one hundred years—and yet most of us resolutely ignore the signs of ageing. This kind of activity is absent from the quiet mind; the quiet mind does not ignore anything.

Initially, it sounds as though the absence of ignorance could be a problem for, if there is no ignoring, it follows that there must be awareness of all kinds of unwelcome things. Indeed there is—but the mind is nevertheless still and quiet.

If we look for a moment at the unquiet mind, the picture may become clearer.

The unquiet mind is always associated with ignorance. If ignorance is doing the job we wish it to do—that is, saving us from all kinds of problems, discomfort and unpleasantness—you might expect that this kind of mind would be quiet, unworried and always happy. This could perhaps be true if ignorance meant simply lack of information, as in the saying 'ignorance is bliss', but it does not; it means, rather, 'wilful avoidance'. The attempted wilful avoidance of the unpleasant creates the 'noise' in the unquiet mind.

Ignorance arises due to craving for things to be different than they are. But, right now, things are as they are and can be no different. The unquiet mind is always tortured by what might be, or what might have been, and never rests content with what is. In complete contrast, the quiet mind has no desire for things to be any different than they are—and is always peaceful and quiet, no matter what is happening.

Such stillness does not imply stasis or deadness, dullness or emotional sterility, nor that there is nothing changing in the quiet mind. Things change, whether we ignore them or whether we do not; and to be content with this—with things as they are—is quite the reverse of stasis. The quiet mind experiences mental and physical change with no resistance. It allows events to unfold at their own pace without trying to get rid of some and to keep others, without trying to hurry them up or slow them down. The quiet mind experiences things as they are. It does not want things to be different, so it does not desire to stop the process of change. The quiet mind still 'lives by Dhamma', as did the Buddha himself. The Buddha said that he took Dhamma as his standard, and indicated that he lived with senses restrained, conscious always of the transient, unsatisfactory and non-self nature of the inner and outer worlds.

In our culture, security is highly prized. We have to be secure and, to that end, are encouraged to take out insurance to cover every aspect of our lives. Some people take out so much insurance that they have difficulty paying for it all and are so 'secure' that living is a burden. The very idea of security is to keep things as they are, to maintain the status quo, and this, when taken to excess, allows no room to breathe or to change. An undue emphasis on safety or security points to an unreasonable fear of change and unrealistic expectations about the future; it is a sign of attempts to ignore reality in favour of a manipulated dream that can only end in disappointment.

The quiet mind is peaceful and still because of the things that are not there, because of the absence of things like ignorance and craving for security. The quiet mind is pure, in the sense that water is pure. The basic structure of water, H_2O, does not change by mixing it with other substances; it remains pure water, with impurities. Remove the foreign matter by filtration or distillation and you have the unchanged pure water. Take out mental impurities like ignorance and craving for things to be different and you are left with pure mind.

The quiet mind is a pure mind, free from stains like ignorance, craving, hatred, dreams, hope and, specifically, ignore-ance. Gone, too, is the view that mind is personal, that it is 'my mind'. Pure mind is not a sort of 'group mind' resulting from 'becoming one with the one', for that would be simply to extend the view of what is personal, to identify with a larger 'self'. The quiet mind is free from any defilement of opinion, of view, of expectation about 'self'.

Being free from view of any kind, the quiet mind is adaptable. It does not cling to the present moment, trying to make it static, nor does it try to drive it away, wishing for something else. It adapts, it flows, it changes with whatever is around; it is pliant and pliable.

Such a mind is beautifully described in the Pali Canon as 'trackless, like a bird through the sky'. A bird flying through the air leaves no track, leaves no mark, leaves nothing by which it can be followed or measured. In the same way, a pure mind leaves no mark of its existence.

The quiet mind leaves no mark for a number of reasons, the most pertinent of which is that, being pure mind, mind without stain, it reflects its surroundings. It is so in tune with its inner and outer environment that it is indistinguishable from them. Meeting with people, for example, pure mind tends to take on their coloration both mentally and, to an extent, in terms of behavioural actions. It acts exactly like a mirror and, to the observer, is effectively invisible. If the observer is a seeker after pure mind, this reflective process makes life extremely difficult, for he sees something that is largely a reflection of himself.

How, then, is it possible for the seeker after truth to discern those of pure mind from whom he or she wishes to learn? What is the process whereby we change ourselves from hopeful, dreaming and ignorant human beings to come eventually to realise the quietness of pure mind?

The process is threefold. First, the worldly mind is transmuted by self-discipline, meditation and study into a mind free from hindrances. Second, the unhindered mind, by developing supramundane insight, beats a path to the gateway to enlightenment. Finally, there is the ultimate leap to enlightenment itself.

The worldly mind has ignorance as its main root, for it is upon this that craving and hatred depend. At this level, ignorance is definitely unawareness of the reality behind the appearances of ordinary life, particularly of the laws governing the mental realm. It is also unawareness of mundane, worldly laws for, based on ignorance, we indulge all kinds of likes and dislikes, cravings and hatreds, and have unrealistic expectations, hopes, fears and dreams. The most obvious characteristic of the worldly mind is that it desires things to be different than they are; it is confused.

The first step is to restrain unwise actions. These include harming other beings, stealing, improper sexual activity, wrong speech and intoxication. Indulging these activities brings in its train nothing but grief and guilt. Restraining these physical activities frees the mind from the problems of guilt or shame that would ordinarily ensue, rendering it quieter and fit for meditation.

The worldly mind's dissatisfaction with the present shows up in activities like craving for more and 'better' things. There may be preoccupation with getting more money or exotic holidays and fine clothes. Such unwise mental behaviour can lead to deep resentment and depression, especially for those without the means to dress in the latest fashionable style, say, or to go out on the town two or three nights a week. The worldly mind suffers greatly under these and many other circumstances. Why? Because it cannot fulfil its expectations, it wants things to be different.

Commonly, those burdened with the worldly mind, unaware of higher truths, maintain that problems they experience are not related to their actions and that their difficulties always stem from a fault in the environment. People complain that the world is treating them unfairly, that the government is wrong for allowing their unemployment and that social security benefits are inadequate. They complain that wages and salaries are too low, that traffic wardens have no compassion or that taxes are too high. People hindered by the worldly mind see many faults in the world at large but rarely if ever question their own behaviour. Holding these views, the only remedy is to make efforts to change the environment—either by political action or revolution, both of which lead to more unrest—or to give in to apathy and boredom. There is seldom any thought of personally adapting to existing circumstances or any thought that the individual himself might be to blame.

The worldly mind's dissatisfaction is also in evidence for those who seek to better themselves. They may try to do this through amassing wealth or possessions, land or property, through politics or through prayer and meditation. Grasping at fame is another, similar endeavour and admiration may be sought through writing letters to the local newspaper, through becoming a famous craftsman or artist, or through the attempt to become a media 'celebrity' or performing artist. Always bound up with self-view, the desire to have more of the things that seem good—or less of the things that are painful—is incontrovertible evidence of wanting things to be different than they are.

Service to others, aid and assistance for those less fortunate than ourselves leads to much satisfaction and happiness. Even here, on this more subtle level, even in such altruistic and entirely beneficial activities, there is worldliness. Many of the efforts involved in trying to make the world a better place stem from craving for things to be different than they are. Where there is craving, the mind is worldly.

The worldly mind is found also in so-called spiritual activities. Here, it may want to be seen as holy or advanced; as making spiritual progress, as superior to others. Based in ignorance of things as they are, the worldly mind is always reaching out for something else, something better, no matter what the field of endeavour.

That, in outline, is the worldly mind. Far from being an unmitigated disaster area, as some believe, it is the very starting point for the journey to the quiet mind, for we can begin the transformation nowhere else.

The worldly mind applies itself to attain a 'better' way of life, whether that means going out on the town one more night a week, studying for a degree or running for office. Eventually, having tried nearly everything, still unsatisfied, it turns its attention to the spiritual field, specifically to prayer or meditation, in the hope of finding there a way to bring an end to dissatisfaction.

Broadly speaking, meditation is designed to transform the ignorance and wrong view at the heart of the worldly mind. With work and growing experience ignorance is lessened and wrong view corrected, bringing the mind more into line with reality by generating greater awareness of what is. Indeed, the search for something better through prayer or meditation already marks a substantial lessening of ignore-ance of the deeper and subtler areas of life. Buddhist meditation, through direct experience, further transforms worldly opinion into what Dhamma calls 'right view', seeing clearly and accurately the way things work.

At the mundane level, this means we come to accept that each of us is responsible for his own actions, that 'actions have results'. This includes the recognition that there is a beneficial result of generosity to the donor and that parents are worthy of great respect for their efforts on our behalf. In addition, mundane right view includes the knowledge that there are other levels of existence where we may be reborn and that there are men and women who know about these things and can show us the way.

At the supramundane level, right view is more refined, going quite beyond ideas of 'beings' being 'reborn'. Here, we come to see that all conditioned mental and physical things are transient, unsatisfactory and non-self. This is not intellectual understanding, but the actual, direct experiencing of these qualities on an ongoing basis. Taken to its ultimate, this insight leads to enlightenment, the destruction of ignorance, craving and hatred and the consequent eradication of suffering. This destruction leaves the mind quiet.

The single purpose of the Buddhist eightfold path is to eliminate suffering, to uncover the quiet mind. It does this by the transmutation of worldly views and opinions into right view, finally to go beyond view altogether. In the process, we come to see that self is but a mental construct, that it has neither ultimate reality nor permanence. We realise that blind adherence to rules and rituals can in no way produce the solution to dissatisfaction. Cutting away reliance upon superstition, the eightfold path cuts away the belief that more and more material things will make us happier.

The acquisition of right view can be seen as getting rid of ten fetters that bind us to suffering. The first three of these are belief in the existence of the self, adherence to rule and ritual, and sceptical doubt about higher things such as the efficacy of meditation and the existence of enlightenment.

The fetters come to be broken by paying meditative attention to things as they are, or at least as near as we can get to things as they are. We pay attention to the internal workings of the mind, to the processes of body, to interactions with our environment, including other people. We begin to see that things are undeniably transient. There is, wherever we look, no permanent object to be found.

We find too that things happen in a completely impersonal manner. Although each of us may believe initially that he is the pivot around which the world turns, meditation soon begins to show this is hardly the case, for the world continues to turn without his express permission. What we believe to be our own decisions, our own actions, are in fact heavily conditioned by the environment in which we move. We have choice or freedom of action only in the most limited of senses.

Today it is thought that everyone has a free choice to do just about whatever he or she wishes and, as far as society is concerned, conventionally speaking, that is of course true. But closely examine any decision, taking into account the preferred responses conditioned by upbringing, education and experience, and invariably we find that there was no other choice possible, given the circumstances at the time. There are only so many ways any one of us can go, given his own particular likes and dislikes, the way he is feeling at the time, the state of the weather and the pressures upon him. What appears to be a free choice is in fact entirely conditioned by various constraining circumstances. Ultimately speaking, there is very little self-direction, as we would normally use the term at the mundane level.

When analysed in this way, it is evident that we do not have free-will or self-choice; what appears to be a free choice at the conventional level is discovered ultimately to be an impersonal conditioning process. Right meditation gradually uncovers this fact and the concept of a separate, permanent self is eroded, bit by bit, simply by observation. This process replaces the wrong view—that there is a lasting, discrete ego-entity—with the right view that there is no permanent, separate self. In this way the first fetter is broken and the process of meditative observation continues eventually to deal with the other fetters, which we do not have time to cover this evening.

The process of meditation transmutes wrong view into right view. Through meditation, we examine craving, hatred and all the other factors we take to be negative. Examining them, we discover them to be based in the wrong views that things are permanent, able to produce happiness and either my self or belonging to my self. In short, craving and hatred can arise only if we are confused and ignorant of the way things really work at the ultimate level.

Craving turns out on reflection to be rather foolish, for several reasons. Craving is an extremely unhappy state, for it focuses on what seems to be lacking here and now. Once acquired, the object of desire always turns out to be less satisfying than imagined—which brings further unhappiness and distress. Even if the object of desire is acceptable, it soon begins to age and decay, it is transient, and trying to cling to it merely accentuates suffering again. Craving begins to look like a stupid activity in which to indulge.

As right view becomes more established, so craving is counteracted by direct knowledge of the ultimately transient—hence unsatisfactory and non-self—nature of things and, in that way, cravings and hatreds diminish.

After much dedicated work, the meditator eventually arrives at the state known as *arahant*. This is generally but mistakenly taken to be synonymous with enlightenment. The *arahant* truly is the acme of perfection with respect to right view. He has fully refined his view structure through observations of the way in which things actually work. Based on correct interpretation of his ultimate meditative experience, his view structure is as accurate as it is possible to be using logic and language. He is not at that point enlightened, however, for he still relies upon his right view and his meditative attainment. At this stage he is at the gateway to enlightenment but has still to pass through.

The meditator has constructed for himself something that the Tibetan school of Buddhism calls a *yidam*. A *yidam* is an image one creates to represent a natural force or quality. The living image is then regarded as a tutelary deity and can indeed teach one much about what it represents. For instance, it could be a personification of compassion, on the positive side, or lust or destructiveness on the negative. It can become so realistically alive that meditators sometimes are terrified by the uncontrollable nature of the entity they have created. Their task is to realise that the image is a creation; it is in no way permanent. It is a concept; an image that has to be transcended before any further progress is possible. This is also the task before the *arahant*.

The *arahant* has fully established right view, and cannot improve upon it. But what do we mean by right view in this context? Right in relation to what? Right view exists only in relation to wrong view; it is one pole of a pair of opposites. Starting from wrong view at one end of the spectrum, the meditator has travelled the entire mental and physical world to arrive at right view at the other—but he or she is still firmly attached to that relative world, however refined. Before enlightenment can occur, right view itself must be given up. Enlightenment is the transcendence of all opposites, including both right and wrong view. The enlightened individual has no view at all. He or she has no view of no view—the question of view or opinion just does not arise. Beyond all opposites, questions of belief, of faith and of hope never arise. They cannot arise, for they are transcended.

The Buddha said that this teaching, Dhamma, was like a raft that you use to ferry yourself across the stream of *saṃsāra*, the mundane world. He asked his monks whether a successful meditator, having reached the opposite bank, should then carry the raft ashore on his back. They naturally replied that such a course of action would be foolish. One would perhaps tie up the raft or sink it in the shallows but certainly not carry it. Leaving it behind one would walk on, free from the burden. In exactly the same way the meditator who has become *arahant* has to leave behind the raft of the teaching and walk away, free even from the teaching itself, free even from right view.

Abandon all view and suddenly the mind is quiet. The tranquil mind is not fixed in any way; it is not fixed to right view and it is certainly not fixed to wrong view. It is not fixed to any view. It does not cling to anything. It does not grasp at or crave for anything at all. The quiet mind is an indistinguishable part of the flux and flow of the surroundings, mental and physical. It does not matter whether there is a raging storm or it is a bright sunny day, the quiet mind accepts the way things are, both externally and internally.

Each of us is conditioned in certain ways and has certain predilections. One wise man was asked why he spent time and effort teaching people when he could have led a quiet and peaceful life. His response was, 'Why does a flower grow?' Refusing to elaborate further, he resumed what he had been saying before the interruption, leaving the student to ponder his words.

It was the perfect answer to the question. A flower grows because it is in a flower's nature to grow. The wise man taught because it was in his nature to teach; he was not fighting his own internal conditioning. Most people believe that to make progress we have to sacrifice ourselves in the forge of meditation and hammer ourselves on the anvil of experience into a totally new shape. That is not the case.

All we have to do—and it is so simple that some find it nearly impossible to start with—is to pay attention to exactly what is present. We do not have to change anything. Any changes that may occur arise naturally from the understanding of mind and body. The most significant of these is the dropping away of expectations built on dissatisfaction, ignorance, craving and hatred. In one way, nothing at all changes—and yet it is a total revolution of the internal world.

We are left with a mind that operates quietly within the compass of existing predilections and preferences—but without any ignorance, craving and hatred. For instance, few of us would choose to stand out in the pouring rain if there was shelter close by—but there need be no craving, hatred or ignorance in the mind to take cover. Most people prefer to brush their teeth in the morning—but it takes no craving to bring it about, merely a preference for a fresh mouth and healthy teeth. Most of us, feeling cold, will put on some extra clothing—but there need be no craving or hatred to do it, simply a preference for warmth. The wise man taught because he preferred to and for no other reason.

★ ★ ★

The quiet mind is the goal of all existence. Every living being that longs to avoid discomfort aims, however indirectly, at enlightenment, the cessation of suffering. We are in effect all on the same path, though of course many are currently lost and bewildered. For a minority in every generation with enough experience of suffering, the causes of distress gradually become more apparent. Those few always spurn conventional goals and set out on the search for true freedom. It is there to be discovered and it is worth any sacrifice one may have to make along the way. The quiet mind is without compare.

Index

All profits from the sale of this book go directly to the Aukana Trust, a registered charity (No 326938) dedicated to the promotion of the Buddha's teaching.

Under the spiritual guidance of **Alan James**, the Aukana Trust provides a wide range of facilities from introductory evening classes in meditation and Buddhist philosophy right through to full-time monastic training. Most of the activities are held at the House of Inner Tranquillity in Bradford on Avon; the Trust also runs classes in London.

If you would like further information, please write to:

Aukana Trust
9 Masons Lane
Bradford on Avon, Wiltshire
BA15 1QN
England

e-mail: aukana@globalnet.co.uk
www.aukana.org.uk

THE UNFOLDING OF WISDOM
The Buddha's Path to Enlightenment

Alan James

' ... it is like having lived all your life in a dark cave, never being sure where the walls, the ceiling or the exits were, never being sure of the real shape of the space around you. When at last you bring in some light to the darkness, immediately your old idea of the cave disappears. The illumination of true vision eliminates what had been total darkness, including all your speculations about the reality of the cave.

'When this occurs, there is never any need to refer to your earlier idea of how things were; it simply becomes irrelevant. Now you know things as they are. What interest can speculative fantasies have for you now?'

The Unfolding of Wisdom is uncompromising. It presents the facts about spiritual progress. It is not for those who would speculate about symbolism or metaphor but for those who would dare to approach truth directly.

ISBN 0 9511769 4 3 (hardback)
    0 9511769 5 1 (softback)

230 x 155mm   224 pages

MODERN BUDDHISM

Alan & Jacqui James

'The Buddha's teaching is as relevant today as it ever has been. It describes the facts of human life which are observable by anyone who cares to take the trouble to investigate.'

Presenting timeless truths in a 20th-century context, *Modern Buddhism* provides answers to questions that have always haunted mankind.

Death and dying: a wasted and terrifying experience—or an opportunity for spiritual growth? A meditation teacher describes the way she helped her mother approach the doors of death.

Family relationships: why do some families live in harmony, whilst others are constantly at war? What is the purpose of the family unit?

Sexuality: what sexual habits are most conducive to progress along the path?

Alan & Jacqui James belong to the tradition of teachers who present the essence of Buddhism in a way which is totally in tune with the needs of their own time and culture.

In a confused and dark world, the book is like a ray of light showing the path to sanity and peace - **Buddhism Today, Brisbane**

ISBN 0 9511769 1 9   *215 x 135mm   176 pages*

BUDDHISM IN A FOREIGN LAND

Robert Mann

As Buddhism is taking root in the West, evolving new forms to suit new conditions, much of its traditional oriental context is being called into question.

In this intriguing and provocative collection of talks, Robert Mann addresses many of the issues which confront Buddhism as it adapts to modern western culture.

Rebirth and traditional cosmology, the role of ethics in 20th-century consumer society, the dangers inherent in confusing therapy with spirituality—these are just some of the topics included in this controversial book.

Covers in an admirably clear manner the fundamentals of the Buddhadharma ... a book to be recommended - **Journal of Buddhist Ethics**

A pleasure to read—lucid, unambiguous and expressive - **Buddhism Now**

ISBN 0 9511769 6 X   *215 x 135mm   192 pages*

LIFE AS A SIAMESE MONK

Richard Randall

May 1954, Bangkok - 10,000 people converge on the outlying temple of Wat Paknam to witness an historic ceremony. 47-year-old journalist Richard Randall is taking the saffron robe to ordain as a Buddhist monk. Known henceforth as Kapilavaddho Bhikkhu, he is the first Englishman to enter the monkhood in Thailand. After an intensive meditation training and some remarkable experiences in concentration and insight practice, Kapilavaddho later went on to play a key role in the introduction of Buddhist meditation to the West.

An exceptionally fine Dhamma-read - **Buddhism Now**

An inspiring story of Buddhist devotion - **Light of Peace, Bangkok**

ISBN 0 9511769 2 7
230 x 150mm   224 pages + 8 pages b/w photographs

BUDDHIST CHARACTER ANALYSIS

Robert Mann & Rose Youd

Food, sleep, relationships, sex: do you go for quality, quantity or moderation? Or would you prefer to live without them?

Buddhist Character Analysis is a practical guide to the infinite complexities of human behaviour.

You're offered your own TV show. Do you think, 'What took them so long?' Or would you rather die?

Based exclusively on observable facts, **Buddhist Character Analysis** identifies our fundamental motives and assumptions.

Does your heart sink at the prospect of a quiet weekend? Or do you believe that the world could be a wonderful place if it wasn't for all those people?

Skilful use of **Buddhist Character Analysis** leads to a greater understanding of human nature and increasing happiness in daily life.

How do you see the enlightened person? An aloof Himalayan hermit, master of self-control? Or a charismatic leader using his powers to create a better world?

Combined with a spiritual training, **Buddhist Character Analysis** deepens insight into the true nature of reality.

A thoroughly readable introduction to the subject - **Holistic London Guide**

ISBN 0 9511769 3 5   *197 x 125mm   144 pages*

BUDDHISM: THE PLAIN FACTS

Robert Mann & Rose Youd

A clear, systematic guide to *vipassana* meditation, the practice of insight at the heart of Buddhism, this book focuses on the original teachings of the Buddha and shows how they can be applied today.

This is Buddhism without history, politics or jargon—the plain facts about the Buddha's path to enlightenment.

ISBN 0 9511769 7 8   *216 x 138mm   176 pages*

Coming soon, a new edition of the meditation classic ...

A MEDITATION RETREAT

Alan & Jacqui James

The Buddha declared that there was just one way to overcome the suffering seemingly inherent in human existence: the practice of mindfulness. This practice generates insight (*vipassana*) into the way our minds work, revealing why we suffer as we do

With a clarity and directness of approach that can only come from understanding, Alan and Jacqui James cover such topics as how to meditate, hindrances to the practice and how to overcome them, the relationship between meditation teacher and student, and enlightenment itself.

While many of these talks were especially designed for the new meditator embarking on his/her first retreat, they will all provide inspiration and a wealth of wisdom for novice and experienced meditator alike.

Based on profound experience and very clearly written ... there is much throughout the book which will prove of benefit to many - **The Middle Way**

Available Autumn 2002

These books are available by mail-order:

Inner Tranquillity	£8.95
The Unfolding of Wisdom	
softback	£8.95
hardback	£10.95
Modern Buddhism	£7.95
Buddhism in a Foreign Land	£8.50
Life as a Siamese Monk	£8.95
Buddhist Character Analysis	£6.95
Buddhism: The Plain Facts	£6.95

Prices include postage and packing

Please send to:

Aukana Trust
9 Masons Lane
Bradford on Avon, Wiltshire
BA15 1QN